# SRA Open Court Reading

# Reteach

## Level 3
### Blackline Masters

A Division of The McGraw-Hill Companies

Columbus, Ohio

**SRA/McGraw-Hill**
*A Division of The McGraw·Hill Companies*

Copyright © 2000 by SRA/McGraw-Hill.

All rights reserved. Except as permitted under the United States Copyright Act, no part of this publication may be reproduced or distributed in any form or by any means, or stored in a database or retrieval system, without the prior written permission of the publisher, unless otherwise indicated.

Send all inquiries to:
SRA/McGraw-Hill
8787 Orion Place
Columbus, OH 43240–4027

Printed in the United States of America.

ISBN 0-02-831104-3

3 4 5 6 7 8 9 DBH 04 03 02 01

# Table of Contents

## Unit 1

| | |
|---|---|
| **Classify and Categorize** | 7 |
| **Point of View** | 9 |
| **Types of Sentences** | 11 |
| **Cause and Effect** | 13 |
| **Plot** | 15 |
| **Compound Words** | 17 |
| **Common and Proper Nouns** | 19 |
| **Drawing Conclusions** | 21 |
| **Characterization** | 23 |
| **Synonyms and Antonyms** | 25 |
| **Adjectives** | 27 |
| **Compare and Contrast** | 29 |
| **Multiple-Meaning Words** | 31 |
| **Dialogue** | 33 |
| **Homonyms** | 35 |
| **Adverbs** | 37 |
| **Sequence** | 39 |
| **Folktales** | 41 |
| **Irregular Plurals** | 43 |
| **Main Idea and Details** | 45 |
| **Contractions** | 47 |
| **Subject-Verb Agreement** | 49 |

## Unit 2

| | |
|---|---|
| **Informational Text** | 51 |
| **Plural Nouns** | 53 |
| **Inflectional Endings** | 55 |
| **Pronoun-Antecedent Agreement** | 57 |
| **Long Vowel Spellings** | 59 |
| **Conjunctions and Compound Sentences** | 61 |
| **Context Clues** | 63 |
| **Present, Past, and Future Tense Verbs** | 65 |
| **Fantasy and Reality** | 67 |

Main Idea and Details ................................................. 69
Fiction and Nonfiction ................................................ 71
Building Vocabulary .................................................. 73
Abbreviations ........................................................... 75
Fact and Opinion ...................................................... 77
Author's Purpose ...................................................... 79
Possessive Nouns ..................................................... 81

## Unit 3

Compare and Contrast ............................................... 83
Short Vowel Sounds .................................................. 85
Multisyllabic Words................................................... 87
Subject and Object Pronouns .................................... 89
Biography ................................................................ 91
Spelling Final *-le* and *-el* ........................................ 93
Author's Point of View............................................... 95
Setting .................................................................... 97
Commas in a Series ................................................. 99
Inflectional Endings ............................................... 101
Subject-Verb Agreement ......................................... 103

## Unit 4

Sequence ............................................................... 105
Author's Purpose .................................................... 107
Classifying and Categorizing .................................. 109
Spellings: Final *-le* and *-el* ................................... 111
Types of Sentences ................................................ 113
Common and Proper Nouns ................................... 115
Dialogue................................................................. 117
Making Inferences ................................................. 119
Synonyms and Antonyms ....................................... 121
Adjectives and Adverbs .......................................... 123

## Unit 5

- Spelling Plural Nouns ............................................. 125
- Irregular Plurals ..................................................... 127
- Author's Point of View............................................ 129
- Commas in a Series ............................................... 131
- Cause and Effect ................................................... 133
- Contractions ......................................................... 135
- Possessive Nouns.................................................. 137
- Drawing Conclusions.............................................. 139
- Building Vocabulary................................................ 141
- Fantasy and Reality ............................................... 143
- Multiple-Meaning Words ......................................... 145
- Punctuating Dialogue.............................................. 147

## Unit 6

- Short and Long Vowel Sounds................................. 149
- Abbreviations ........................................................ 151
- Fact and Opinion ................................................... 153
- Figurative Language ............................................... 155
- Pronouns .............................................................. 157
- Context Clues........................................................ 159
- Conjunctions ......................................................... 161
- Making Inferences.................................................. 163
- Compound Words................................................... 165
- Verbs ................................................................... 167
- Homonyms ........................................................... 169
- Subject and Object Pronouns................................... 171
- Multisyllabic Words ................................................ 173

Name _____   Date _____

# Classify and Categorize

*Gloria Who Might Be My Best Friend*

**Focus** **Classifying and categorizing** means putting things into groups.

> Readers sort information into different groups, or **categories**. This helps them to understand and remember what they read.

**Practice** Think about the items in the box. Then, answer the questions below.

| bananas | green beans | apples |
|---------|-------------|--------|
| corn    | oranges     | carrots |

Which of the items in the box are fruits? _____

_____

Which of the items in the box are vegetables? _____

_____

List the items under the correct category.

| Fruits | Vegetables |
|--------|------------|
| _____ | _____ |
| _____ | _____ |
| _____ | _____ |

**Reteach** • *Classify/Categorize*

**Classify and Categorize** *(continued)*

The things in the box below can be found at a circus. They can be divided into two categories: people and food. Place each item from the box under its correct category.

---

| popcorn | clowns | cotton candy |
| acrobats | jugglers | hot dogs |

---

**People**                                      **Food**

_____         _____

_____         _____

_____         _____

**Apply** Suppose your family is going to move to a new city. Think of one category of things that you will need to move, such as clothing, toys, or furniture. Write down three things from that category that you would need to put in a box.

Category: _____

_____

Items: _____

_____

Name _____   Date _____

# Point of View

*Gloria Who Might Be My Best Friend*

**Focus** Point of view is the position or viewpoint from which a story is told. A story is told from a **first-person point of view** or a **third-person point of view**.

---

**First-Person Point of View**

- The storyteller is a character in the story. The storyteller tells about his or her own thoughts or feelings.

- The storyteller uses the words *I, me, we, our,* and *us*.

**Third-Person Point of View**

- The storyteller is not a character in the story. The storyteller tells about things that happen to people in the story.

- The storyteller uses the words *he, she, him, her, they, their,* and *them*.

---

**Practice** Read each sentence or sentence pair. Notice the underlined pronouns. Write which point of view the storyteller is using. Is it first-person point of view or third-person point of view?

1. <u>I</u> tiptoed into the den and turned on the light.

   _____

2. The prince rode his horse to the village.
   <u>He</u> was looking for the princess.

   _____

Reteach • *Point of View*     9

**Point of View** *(continued)*

3. The puppy put her paw on the boy's lap. <u>She</u> was looking for a home.

   _____

4. When <u>I</u> saw the crowd, <u>I</u> knew there was something wrong.

   _____

5. <u>I</u> jumped on the horse's back and rode it out into the pasture.

   _____


**Apply** Write one sentence from the first-person point of view and another sentence from the third-person point of view.

first-person point of view: _____

_____

_____

third-person point of view: _____

_____

_____

Name _____  Date _____

# Types of Sentences

*Gloria Who Might Be My Best Friend*

**Focus** Writers use different kinds of sentences to make stories more interesting.

---

- A **statement** tells something and ends with a **period**.
   I know the best way to make wishes.

- A **question** asks something and ends with a **question mark**.
   How many wishes did you make?

- A sentence that shows strong feeling ends with an **exclamation point** and is called an **exclamation**.
   My wish came true!

---

**Practice** Read the following sentences. Decide whether each sentence is a question, a statement, or an exclamation. Circle the correct answer.

1. Can we go to the play with them?

    statement        question        exclamation

2. My dance teacher said I was doing a good job.

    statement        question        exclamation

3. That is a beautiful picture!

    statement        question        exclamation

4. I am happy to make you a new folder.

    statement        question        exclamation

Reteach • *Types of Sentences*

**Types of Sentences** (continued)

Add the correct punctuation to each of the following sentences.

5. Today is Haley's birthday_____

6. Haley likes chocolate cake_____

7. Wow, look at that cake_____

8. How many layers does it have_____

9. Who made it_____

10. Aunt Sue made it_____

11. Thanks, Aunt Sue_____

12. Are you going to have a piece_____

13. This cake tastes great_____

14. Can I please have another piece_____

15. Will there be any cake left for tomorrow_____

**Apply** Write either a statement, a question, or an exclamation about a special celebration.

_____

_____

_____

Name _____  Date _____

# Cause and Effect

*Angel Child, Dragon Child*

**Focus** Looking for causes and effects helps you to better understand story events.

- A **cause** is why something happens.
- An **effect** is what happens as a result.

**Practice** Read each sentence below. Then, answer the questions. The first one is done for you.

1. The teacher called on Iris because Iris had her hand up.

    What happened? **The teacher called on Iris.**

    Why did it happen? **Iris had her hand up.**

2. The tire went flat because Dad ran over a nail.

    What happened? _____

    Why did it happen? _____

3. The ground was wet because it rained.

    What happened? _____

    Why did it happen? _____

4. I studied because I had a test.

    What happened? _____

    Why did it happen? _____

Reteach • *Cause and Effect*

**Cause and Effect** (continued)

Read each sentence. Write the effect (what happened) and the cause (why the effect happened) in each sentence.

5. I was tired, so I went to bed.

   Effect: _____

   Cause: _____

6. I drank milk because we had no juice.

   Effect: _____

   Cause: _____

7. The electricity went off because there was a storm.

   Effect: _____

   Cause: _____

8. The cookies burned, so I threw them away.

   Effect: _____

   Cause: _____

9. The dog's paws were muddy, so I put him in the garage.

   Effect: _____

   Cause: _____

**Apply** Write a cause-and-effect sentence about losing your lunch money.

_____

_____

Name _____   Date _____

# Plot

**Focus** The plot is made up of the things that happen in the story.

---

**Parts of a Plot**

- A story has a beginning, a middle, and an end.
- The characters have a problem, which is usually told at the beginning of the story.
- The characters' struggles lead to a high point, or climax.
- The story comes to a conclusion, which is usually the solution to the problem.

---

**Practice and Apply** Read the story and answer the questions.

    Once upon a time there was a dragon who lived alone in a cave. He was a good dragon even though he did breathe fire. He wanted to have a friend. This dragon would go out in the countryside every day looking for a friend. He became sad after many weeks of looking. One day, a boy who was lost was crying on a hill near the cave. The dragon heard him and walked over. He got the boy to stop crying, and the two became good friends.

Setting: Where does the story take place?

1. _____

Main character: Who is the main character of this story?

2. _____

Reteach • *Plot*

**Plot** *(continued)*

Problem: What is the problem?

3. _____

Solution: What is the solution to the problem?

4. _____


Read the following story. Then, answer the questions.

    Timmy went to the zoo. He saw many animals. Timmy wanted to buy some popcorn. He didn't have any money. Timmy spotted a coin on the ground. He used the coin to buy some popcorn.

Setting: Where does the story take place?

1. _____

Main character: Who is the main character of this story?

2. _____

Problem: What is the problem?

3. _____

Climax: What is the climax or high point?

4. _____

Solution: What is the solution to the problem?

5. _____

Name _____   Date _____

# Compound Words

*Angel Child, Dragon Child*

**Focus** Using compound words can make your writing more interesting.

> A **compound word** is one word that is made of two words joined together.
>
> match + box = matchbox     a box of matches
> wind + storm = windstorm     a storm with wind
> corn + bread = cornbread     bread made of corn

**Practice** Complete each compound word equation. Then, write the meaning of the compound word.

1. side + _____ = sidewalk

   Meaning: _____

2. swing + set = _____

   Meaning: _____

3. _____ + shell = seashell

   Meaning: _____

4. _____ + _____ = moonlight

   Meaning: _____

5. _____ + _____ = mailbox

   Meaning: _____

Reteach • *Compound Words*

**Compound Words** (continued)

6. _____ + book = schoolbook

   Meaning: _____

7. _____ + _____ = skateboard

   Meaning: _____

8. pop + _____ = popcorn

   Meaning: _____

9. rattle + _____ = rattlesnake

   Meaning: _____

10. _____ + _____ = bookshelf

    Meaning: _____

11. _____ + _____ = fireplace

    Meaning: _____

12. _____ + _____ = teacup

    Meaning: _____

13. _____ + _____ = wristwatch

    Meaning: _____

**Apply** Write a sentence using a compound word of your own.

_____

_____

_____

Name _____   Date _____

# Common and Proper Nouns

*Angel Child, Dragon Child*

**Focus** A **noun** is a word that names a person, place, or thing.

- A **common noun** names **any** person, place, or thing. Common nouns begin with a **lowercase letter**.

- A **proper noun** names a **particular** person, place, or thing. Proper nouns always begin with a **capital letter**.

| Kind of Noun | Common Noun | Proper Noun |
|---|---|---|
| person | girl | Rachel |
| place | country | Spain |
| thing | bridge | Golden Gate Bridge |

**Practice** Write each of the following nouns in the correct column.

| student | United States | Atlantic Ocean | festival |
|---|---|---|---|
| state | Monday | Memorial Day | carrot |

**Common Nouns**            **Proper Nouns**

_____       _____

_____       _____

_____       _____

_____       _____

Reteach • *Common and Proper Nouns*                    **19**

**Common and Proper Nouns** *(continued)*

**Apply** Read the sentences below. Write a proper noun in each blank.

1. My name is _____.

2. I live on _____ Street.

3. I have three sisters named _____, _____, and _____.

4. My pet's name is _____.

5. My favorite holiday is _____.

6. I like to go to _____ on vacation.

7. One state I have never visited is _____.

8. My best friend's name is _____.

9. The name of my school is _____.

10. My teacher's name is _____.

11. My favorite cartoon character is _____.

12. My favorite book is _____.

13. A country I have never visited is _____.

14. My principal's name is _____.

Name _____  Date _____

# Drawing Conclusions

*Stevie*

**Focus** By using clues from the story, readers can draw conclusions about what they've read.

> - To **draw a conclusion** means to make a statement about a character or event by putting together small details about that character or event.
> - A conclusion may not be stated in the text, but it should be supported by examples from the text.

**Practice** Read the sentences. Place a check mark next to each sentence that supports the conclusion that Robert does not like Stevie.

_____ 1. Stevie is younger.

_____ 2. Sometimes, Stevie was fun to play with.

_____ 3. Stevie was only around for a little while.

_____ 4. Even after I told him not to, Stevie kept playing with my stuff.

_____ 5. Stevie was very little.

_____ 6. I miss Stevie. He was a nice guy.

_____ 7. Stevie was always making lots of noise and getting me in trouble.

_____ 8. Because of Stevie, I couldn't even play with my friends.

_____ 9. Stevie was kind of like a little brother.

_____ 10. I had lots of fun until Stevie came to stay with us.

Reteach • *Drawing Conclusions*

**Drawing Conclusions** *(continued)*

Read the sentences below. Then, use what they tell you to draw a conclusion.

- Firefighters put out fires.
- Firefighters check the hoses.
- Firefighters clean the fire trucks.
- Firefighters talk to schoolchildren about safety.
- Firefighters save lives.

Conclusion: _____

_____

**Apply** Read the paragraph. Write a conclusion for it on the lines below.

    Jason and Tony play on the same soccer team. They both have Mrs. Myers for their third-grade teacher, and they live on the same street. Both like to swim and fish, and each has a younger sister.

_____

_____

_____

_____

Name _____ Date _____

# Characterization

*Stevie*

**Focus** The more you know about characters in a story, the more you can understand and enjoy the story.

> Writers create **characterization** by
> - using the characters' words.
> - showing the characters' actions.
> - showing how the characters react to each other.

**Practice and Apply** Read the paragraphs below. Complete the character web on the next page by writing words or phrases that describe Thomas.

> The class had been hiking for a long time.
> "Do you think we'll ever get there?" Mark said. "I don't think I can walk another step." Mark dropped his backpack on the path. Then, he sat down on a rock.
> Thomas turned around. "We don't have far to go. Just hang in there. Can I help you carry anything?"
> "Maybe you can carry my water bottle," Mark said. "It's heavy."
> Thomas took Mark's water bottle. Thomas helped Mark put his backpack on.
> "I'll be right behind you, Mark. Hey, let's sing!" The boys joined the class, marching and singing along the path.

Reteach • *Characterization*

**Characterization** *(continued)*

**What Thomas says:**
_____
_____
_____

**Thomas**

**What Thomas does:**
_____
_____
_____
_____
_____

**How Thomas treats others:**
_____
_____
_____

Name _____    Date _____

# Synonyms and Antonyms

*Stevie*

**Focus** You can use synonyms and antonyms to make your writing more interesting and to say exactly what you mean.

> A **synonym** is a word that means almost the same thing as another word. *Little* and *small* are synonyms.
>
> An **antonym** is a word that means the opposite of another word. *Hot* and *cold* are antonyms.

**Practice** Match the words in Column 1 with their *synonyms* in Column 2.

| Column 1 | Column 2 |
|---|---|
| find | idea |
| fasten | locate |
| fearful | enjoy |
| thought | hook |
| boring | limb |
| branch | dull |
| like | scared |
| car | end |
| close | leave |
| go | shut |
| finish | auto |

**Reteach** • *Synonyms and Antonyms*

25

**Synonyms and Antonyms** (continued)

Match the words in Column A with their *antonyms* in Column B.

| Column A | Column B |
|---|---|
| difficult | laugh |
| silly | lazy |
| cry | common |
| hard-working | serious |
| bright | easy |
| rare | dull |

**Apply** Write a sentence that describes a house, using the word *bright*. Then write the sentence again, replacing *bright* with the antonym *dark*.

1. _____

2. _____

Name _____  Date _____

# Adjectives

Stevie

**Focus** To describe people, places, or things, you use adjectives.

> An **adjective** is a word that describes a noun. It tells which one, how many, or what kind.
>   The **red** car          My **kind** sister
>   Our **new** home      The **little** park

**Practice** Read the sentences. Circle the adjective that describes the underlined noun.

1. The frightened boy cried.

2. The tall tree gives shade.

3. A lone star shines in the sky.

4. We chose the brown puppy.

5. Martha rode the blue bike.

6. A big icicle hangs from the roof.

7. The green frog jumped into the pond.

8. The white cat played in the sun.

9. Can you find the small scissors?

10. Rosa eats the warm taco.

11. I am carrying three books.

12. The tiny baby smiled at me.

**Reteach** • *Adjectives*

**Adjectives** (continued)

Complete the sentences with adjectives from the box.

| great | prettiest | muddy | happy |
| one | deep | fresh | new |

13. The _____ fruit tasted good!

14. _____ ice cream cone for dessert is enough.

15. Her _____ shoes tracked dirt across the floor.

16. It was a _____ day for a picnic.

17. The _____ child began to laugh.

18. The _____ seashell was Martha's.

19. I got a _____ bike for my birthday.

20. The _____ end of the pool was cold!

**Apply** Write adjectives to complete each sentence.

1. The _____ kite floats in the _____ sky.

2. The _____ clown wore a _____ hat.

3. My _____ brother gave me a _____ book.

4. The _____ frog leaped into the _____ lake.

Adjectives • Reteach

Name _____    Date _____

# Compare and Contrast

*Priscilla, Meet Felicity*

**Focus** When writers tell how two or more things are alike or different, they are comparing. When writers tell how two or more things are different, they are contrasting.

> **Comparing** means telling how two or more things are **alike** or **different**.
> **Contrasting** means telling how two or more things are **different**.

**Practice** Look at the pictures. Then, answer the questions below.

1. Which animal is larger? _____

2. Which animal is smaller? _____

3. Which animal has longer fur? _____

4. Which animal has shorter fur? _____

5. Which animal weighs less? _____

6. Which animal weighs more? _____

Reteach • *Compare and Contrast*

**Compare and Contrast** *(continued)*

**Apply** Read each pair of items. Explain how the items are alike and how they are different. The first one is done for you.

1. a car and a bus

    How are they alike? __They both have wheels and use gas. They both carry people and are used for travel.__

    How are they different? __A car is smaller than a bus and carries fewer people.__

2. a tree and a flower

    How are they alike? _____

    _____

    How are they different? _____

    _____

3. an orange and an apple

    How are they alike? _____

    _____

    How are they different? _____

    _____

Name _____   Date _____

# Multiple-Meaning Words

*Priscilla, Meet Felicity*

**Focus** Some words are confusing because they have more than one meaning.

---

Some words have more than one meaning.
**light**   1. not heavy
            2. something we use to see

Sam's book bag is **light**. (meaning 1)
The **light** in the garage burned out. (meaning 2)

---

**Practice** Read each sentence below, noting the underlined word. Then, circle the definition that best matches the meaning of the underlined word.

1. The girl lost her turn because she did not play fair.
   a) treating everyone alike
   b) sunny
   c) following the rules

2. Rosa skinned her knee on the rough bark of the oak log.
   a) the outside covering of a tree trunk
   b) a sound that a dog makes
   c) to speak in a mean, loud manner

3. The slice of fresh-baked bread had strawberry jam on it.
   a) a spread made out of fruit and sugar
   b) a difficult problem
   c) to push or squeeze together

4. From the plane, Chris saw his aunt wave good-bye.
   a) to sway
   b) to move the hand in signal
   c) a moving ridge of water

Reteach • *Multiple-Meaning Words*

**Multiple-Meaning Words** (continued)

**Apply** Read the definitions for each word in the box. Write the number of the definition that best matches the meaning of the word in each sentence.

| | |
|---|---|
| bark | 1. hard outside covering of a tree |
| | 2. the sound a dog makes |
| tie | 1. to fasten together with string |
| | 2. a cloth worn around the neck |
| pen | 1. a writing instrument |
| | 2. a small space for animals to live in |
| bowl | 1. a rounded dish |
| | 2. to play the game of bowling |
| duck | 1. a large wild bird |
| | 2. to lower quickly |

_____ 1. The dog will bark when the doorbell rings.

_____ 2. The bark of the tree was peeling off.

_____ 3. Dad's new tie was his favorite present.

_____ 4. Please tie your shoes before you go outside.

_____ 5. Did the pen fall on the floor?

_____ 6. The pigs are in their pen.

_____ 7. My dad likes to bowl.

_____ 8. I eat my cereal in a bowl.

_____ 9. He had to duck to avoid being hit.

_____ 10. The duck ate the bread we gave him.

Name _____  Date _____

# Dialogue

*The Tree House*

**Focus** Dialogue is talk between characters in a story.

- **Quotation marks** show the words that characters say.
- Dialogue helps make characters seem real.
- Dialogue helps move the action of the story along.

**Practice** Read the passage. Put quotation marks at the beginning and end of each line of dialogue. Underline the words that tell who is speaking.

Today we are going on a field trip, said the teacher. We are going to the zoo. Is everyone ready?

Sally asked, Should we bring our lunches?

Yes, you should, answered the teacher. We will be at the zoo during our lunchtime.

I hope we see the monkeys this time, thought Mike.

May we feed the animals? asked Dawn.

No, said the teacher. The animals will get sick eating our food.

I see the bus coming, said Scott.

Reteach • *Dialogue*  33

**Dialogue** (continued)

**Apply** Read the following passage. Underline what Mother says. Then, answer the questions.

Tobias said, "I need a note so that I can go on the class field trip."

"Where is the class going?" Mother asked.

"I forget," Tobias mumbled.

"How do you know you want to go if you don't remember where you are going? Tobias, you've been forgetful lately," Mother said.

Ten minutes later, Tobias burst into the kitchen. "I found the flyer that tells about the field trip. Now, I really want to go!" Tobias said.

"Where is the class going?" Mother repeated her earlier question.

"We're going to the museum where you work, Mom!"

1. What does Mother ask Tobias?
   _____
   _____

2. What dialogue tells you where Mother works?
   _____
   _____

Name _____  Date _____

# Homonyms

*The Tree House*

**Focus** A homonym is a word that sounds the same as another word but has a different meaning and spelling.

Here are some homonyms you know.

| | | |
|---|---|---|
| by | buy | A tree is <u>by</u> the house.<br>Did Bob <u>buy</u> a new book? |
| some | sum | The cat drank <u>some</u> milk.<br>The <u>sum</u> of 3 and 3 is 6. |
| hole | whole | The rabbit dug a <u>hole</u>.<br>Sam ate the <u>whole</u> melon. |
| so | sew | Do not walk <u>so</u> fast.<br>I'll <u>sew</u> the button on. |
| through | threw | I peeked <u>through</u> a crack.<br>Jose <u>threw</u> the ball to me. |
| meet | meat | <u>Meet</u> me at ten o'clock.<br>Steve grilled the <u>meat</u>. |
| eye | I | Dolly shut one <u>eye</u>.<br><u>I</u> cannot see you. |
| one | won | Tyrone had <u>one</u> ticket.<br>My calf <u>won</u> a red ribbon. |

**Practice** Read each sentence. Then, underline the word that completes it.

1. The puppy looked out (threw, through) the screen door.

2. Margie put (some, sum) pictures on the wall.

3. The family has (bin, been) away on vacation.

Reteach • *Homonyms*  35

**Homonyms** (continued)

4. Carlos will slice (meet, meat) to make a sandwich.

5. Tran lives in a city (by, buy) the ocean.

6. Dad dug a (hole, whole) and planted the tree.

7. We walked out (through, threw) the back door.

8. My team (one, won) the game.

9. Mother took me to (by, buy) new shoes.

10. Jess will (meet, meat) you in front of the school.

11. She just has (one, won) more question.

12. The pitcher (through, threw) her best pitch.

13. When you add, the answer is the (some, sum).

**Apply** Choose one of the following pairs of homonyms. Then write two sentences, using one of the words in each sentence.

| eye / I | so / sew |

1. _____

2. _____

Name _____   Date _____

# Adverbs

**The Tree House**

**Focus** Adverbs describe verbs. Adverbs usually tell when, where, how, or how often. Many end in *-ly*.

> **Adverbs** answer the question *How? How often? When?* or *Where?*
> 
> The test is <u>today</u>. (when)
> The bugs are <u>everywhere</u>. (where)
> She <u>quietly</u> opened the door. (how)
> He <u>always</u> reads in bed. (how often)

**Practice** Read the sentences. Circle the adverb used in each sentence. The questions help you think about which word tells how, how often, when, or where.

1. We did our homework quickly. (How did we do our homework?)

2. We waited outside for our friend. (Where did we wait?)

3. We visit the library weekly. (How often do we visit the library?)

4. A cat waits patiently by the door. (How does the cat wait?)

5. I'll call you soon. (When will I call?)

6. Alicia never takes naps. (How often does Alicia take naps?)

Underline each adverb. Write *how, when, where,* or *how often*.

7. Molly goes to bed early.   _____

8. John talked quietly.   _____

Reteach • *Adverbs*   37

**Adverbs** (continued)

9. It is time to leave now. _____

10. I saw puddles everywhere. _____

11. Bill never misses a day of school. _____

12. I walked slowly up the stairs. _____

13. Here are the missing books! _____

14. Mother and I sometimes sit in the park. _____

15. Can you call me tomorrow? _____

16. The cat swiftly climbed the tree. _____

17. Another student worked nearby. _____

18. Chris stayed inside for a long time. _____

19. Don't look up! _____

**Apply** The words in the box are adverbs. Write each word under a heading to show if the word tells *how*, *when*, or *where*.

| away | soon | late |
| slowly | here | fast |
| there | loudly | yesterday |

**How?**   **When?**   **Where?**

_____   _____   _____

_____   _____   _____

_____   _____   _____

Adverbs • Reteach

Name _____  Date _____

# Sequence

**Focus** The more you know about when things happen in a story and the order in which they happen, the better you can understand the story. When things happen and the order in which they happen is called **sequence**.

*How Dog Outwitted Leopard*

> Some words tell what **time** or when things happen.
> *once    today    before    after    tonight*
>
> Some words tell the **order** in which things happen.
> *first    second    next    last    finally*

**Practice** The following sentences are not in order. Use the time and order words to number them in the correct order.

1. _____ Finally, I had my shoes.

   _____ After five minutes of searching, they were still missing.

   _____ First, I could not find my shoes.

2. _____ Next, I asked Sacha for paper.

   _____ Before starting my homework, I asked Hannah for a pencil.

   _____ At last, I could begin my homework.

3. _____ Yesterday, I took the bus to school.

   _____ I am planning to take my bike tomorrow.

   _____ Today, I walked to school.

Reteach • *Sequence*

**Sequence** (*continued*)

Use the words in the box to complete the following sentences.

| then | first | tomorrow | finally |
| before | yesterday | last | |

4. _____ I visit the dentist, I will brush my teeth.

5. Lucy scored an "A" on her test _____ by studying for a week.

6. Our class plans to go on a trip to the zoo _____.

7. The _____ person to leave the room should turn off the lights.

8. We went to the mall. _____ we went to the movies.

9. My grandmother was the _____ female doctor in our town.

10. After hours of work, we were _____ finished.

**Apply** Write a sentence using a time word.

_____

_____

Name _____  Date _____

# Folktales

**How Dog Outwitted Leopard**

**Focus** A folktale is an old story that has been passed on from person to person for many years.

> **Folktales** often include
> - unusual characters, such as animals or objects that speak.
> - a lesson or moral.
> - an explanation of why things are the way they are.

**Practice and Apply** Read each paragraph below and decide if it is part of a folktale. Write *yes* or *no* on the line. If you write *yes*, underline any clues that helped you make this decision.

1. The giant panda is an animal that is related to the raccoon. It lives in China. The giant panda eats eucalyptus leaves. _____

2. The fox looked up at the crow and said, "What a beautiful voice you have." The crow began to sing. _____

3. Donald and his grandfather went to the beach. They built a sand castle and went swimming. _____

Reteach • *Folktales*

**Folktales** (continued)

4. The little girl thought she heard someone yelling. She looked around, but all she saw was a green frog on the road. She bent down to look closely at the frog. "Will you help me?" begged the frog. _____

5. Mother Hen was busy feeding her chicks, when all of a sudden a strong wind started. "Run, run, run inside the chicken coop," she said to her chicks. _____

6. The baseball field was brand new. The team was warming up for their first game of the season. The stands were full of parents and friends. _____

7. The three pigs told the wolf, "You can't blow our house down." The wolf answered, "I'll huff and puff and blow your house down." _____

8. Mrs. Kennedy drove to the grocery store where she bought milk, flour, eggs, sugar, and chocolate frosting. She was baking a cake for Larry's birthday. _____

Name _____  Date _____

# Irregular Plurals

*How Dog Outwitted Leopard*

**Focus** A plural noun is a noun that names more than one of a person, place, or thing. The plural form of some nouns is irregular.

---

The spelling of some singular nouns must be changed to make them plural.

| Singular | Plural |
|---|---|
| foot | feet |
| ox | oxen |

A few nouns have the same singular and plural forms.

| Singular | Plural |
|---|---|
| reindeer | reindeer |
| moose | moose |
| deer | deer |
| spacecraft | spacecraft |

---

**Practice** Circle the correct plural form of each word.

1. mice        mouses
2. mans        men
3. foots       feet
4. spacecraft  spacecrafts
5. women       womans
6. tooths      teeth
7. children    childs
8. reindeer    reindeers

Reteach • *Irregular Plurals*

**Irregular Plurals** (continued)

Circle the correct plural noun needed to complete the sentence.

9. The (childs, children) were studying about animals in school.

10. They learned that (deer, deers) have antlers.

11. Some (moose, mooses) have antlers, too.

12. (Gooses, Geese) migrate in the winter.

13. People get wool from (sheep, sheeps).

14. (Oxes, Oxen) were used to pull wagons.

15. Many (mouses, mice) live in barns and fields.

16. A herd of (reindeers, reindeer) can be frightened by wolves.

17. A puppy's (teeth, tooths) are small and sharp.

**Apply** There are four incorrect plurals in the paragraph below. Circle the incorrect plural and rewrite the correct plural above it.

All the childs saw the goose run for the pond. Two woman and two man gave them bread to eat. Soon, the bread was all gone.

Name _____     Date _____

# Main Idea and Details

Teammates

**Focus** The **main idea** of a paragraph tells what the paragraph is about.

- The **main idea** is often, but not always, the first sentence of a paragraph. Placing the main idea first helps readers know what the paragraph is about.

- A paragraph is a group of sentences that tells about one idea. The other sentences in the paragraph tell about the main idea. These are called **detail sentences**.

**Practice** Read each paragraph. Then, read the sentences that follow. Put a check by the sentence that tells the main idea of the paragraph.

1. Thousands of people visit Yellowstone National Park each year. People come to see the geysers and the buffalo. They like to hike on the trails and enjoy the beautiful landscapes.

    _____ Yellowstone National Park has buffalo.

    _____ Yellowstone National Park is a favorite vacation spot for many people.

    _____ Yellowstone National Park is located in Wyoming.

Reteach • *Main Idea and Supporting Details*     45

**Main Idea and Details** (continued)

2. After nine innings, the score was tied and it was my turn at bat. Our team had two outs. If I struck out, the game would go into extra innings. I swung and heard the sound of the ball hitting the bat. I watched the ball soar over the fence!

   _____ We played baseball.

   _____ Baseball is a sport.

   _____ My baseball game was exciting.

3. We saw elephants and snakes and watched the dolphin show. Most of the class really liked the monkeys. My favorite animals were the polar bears.

   _____ Our class took a field trip to the zoo.

   _____ The zoo has polar bears.

   _____ The giraffe ate the tree leaves.

**Apply** Read the following paragraph. Underline the main idea.

Caring for a pet involves many things. You must feed your pet every day and make sure it has fresh water at all times. You must exercise your pet and make sure it has regular visits to the vet.

Name _____    Date _____

# Contractions

*Teammates*

**Focus** Sometimes writers use shortcuts when they write.

- A **contraction** is a word made by joining two words. When the words are joined, one or more letters are left out. An **apostrophe** (') takes the place of the missing letter or letters.
  <u>She is</u> late for dinner.   <u>She's</u> late for dinner.
- Here are some word pairs and their contractions.
  we are    we're       they are     they're
  I will    I'll        could not    couldn't

**Practice** Match the pair of words to its contraction. Write the letter of the contraction on the line.

_____  1. do not       a. weren't
_____  2. you have     b. I'll
_____  3. they have    c. don't
_____  4. does not     d. there's
_____  5. he would     e. wasn't
_____  6. I will       f. they've
_____  7. were not     g. I'd
_____  8. there is     h. doesn't
_____  9. was not      i. you've
_____  10. I had       j. he'd

Reteach • *Contractions*

**Contractions** (continued)

Underline the contraction in each sentence. Write the word pair that makes up each contraction.

11. My class isn't going outside for recess. _____

12. We're staying inside to work on our projects. _____

13. We couldn't work on them yesterday. _____

14. The projects look hard, but they aren't. _____

15. They're really fun! _____

16. We'll be finished tomorrow. _____

**Apply** Rewrite the underlined words as a contraction using the words in the box.

| didn't    There's    won't    doesn't    don't |

1. Linda does not like fish. _____

2. There is enough for everyone to share. _____

3. I do not want to go to the store today. _____

4. If she did not want the soup, why did she take it? _____

5. David will not be coming to the meeting. _____

Name _____  Date _____

# Subject-Verb Agreement

*Teammates*

**Focus** The verb must agree with the subject of the sentence.

> Every sentence has a subject and a verb.
>
> - If the subject is singular, then the verb must be singular. Singular verbs end in *-s*.
>   The <u>girl runs</u> around the track.
>
> - If the subject is plural, then the verb must be plural. Plural verbs do not end in *-s*.
>   The <u>girls run</u> around the track.

**Practice** Underline the correct verb in each sentence.

1. Maria and Tamara (do, does) many activities together.

2. Maria (take, takes) gymnastic lessons with Tamara.

3. They (practice, practices) on the equipment.

4. Tamara and Maria (play, plays) baseball, too.

5. Tamara (pitch, pitches) for the team.

6. They (like, likes) playing baseball.

7. Tamara also (like, likes) to read books about horses.

8. She (want, wants) to have her own horse.

Reteach • *Subject-Verb Agreement*

**Subject-Verb Agreement** (continued)

Read the sentences. If the subject and verb agree, write *yes*. If they do not, write *no*.

_____ 9. The celebration lasts all evening.

_____ 10. Families enjoy the special day.

_____ 11. People dances and has fun.

_____ 12. Children plays games.

_____ 13. Many boys and girls win prizes.

**Apply** On each line, write the verb that correctly completes the sentence.

1. Sarah _____ on the new computer. (type, types)

2. Mom _____ our dinner every night. (cook, cooks)

3. The baby _____ juice from a cup. (drink, drinks)

4. When can we _____ to school? (walk, walks)

5. Stu and Doug _____ up the mountain trail. (hike, hikes)

6. His sister _____ the puzzle to her friends. (show, shows)

Name _____  Date _____

# Informational Text

*City Critters*

**Focus** The more information you have about the events in a story, the more likely you are to understand the story.

> **Informational text**
> - is nonfiction.
> - contains facts about real events or real people.
> - gives events in the order in which they happen.
> - may be organized by topics.
> - may contain photographs or diagrams.

**Practice** Read each paragraph and answer the questions.

1. There are more than 350 different kinds of sharks. The dwarf shark is small enough to fit in the palm of your hand. The whale shark is bigger than a school bus. Some sharks have stripes like tigers, and others have heads like a hammer.

   Is this paragraph fiction or nonfiction? _____

   What clues helped you decide? _____

   _____

   _____

2. Dogs make great pets, but they are also used for important jobs. Seeing Eye dogs are specially trained dogs that help people who are blind. Some dogs help police officers and firefighters locate people. Farmers

Reteach • *Informational Text*

**Informational Text** *(continued)*

may use dogs to watch over cattle and sheep. In World War II dogs even found wounded soldiers and carried messages.

Is this paragraph fiction or nonfiction? _____

What clues helped you decide? _____

_____

_____

3. Sam walked to the end of the street. Where was Jake? He was supposed to have met Sam 15 minutes ago. "That's it," thought Sam. "I'm not waiting one second longer." Sam carefully picked up the box and started walking to the fort.

Is this paragraph fiction or nonfiction? _____

What clues helped you decide? _____

_____

_____

**Apply** Read the passage. Then, answer the questions.

In 1622, a ship named the *Atocha* sank near the coast of Florida. The *Atocha* was a Spanish treasure ship packed with gold, jewels, and silver bars. Hurricane winds and powerful ocean currents scattered the treasure.

1. When did the event happen? _____

2. Where did the event happen? _____

3. What happened to the *Atocha*? _____

Name _____   Date _____

# Plural Nouns

*City Critters*

**Focus** A noun that stands for more than one person, place, or thing is **plural**.

> Add -*s* to the ends of most nouns to form the plural.
>    hat ⟶ hat<u>s</u>          book ⟶ book<u>s</u>
>
> Add -*es* to nouns ending in *s*, *ss*, *x*, *ch*, or *sh*.
>    crutch ⟶ crutch<u>es</u>     fox ⟶ fox<u>es</u>
>    dress ⟶ dress<u>es</u>       dish ⟶ dish<u>es</u>
>
> Change the *y* to *i* and add -*es* to nouns that end in a consonant and *y*.
>    hobby ⟶ hobb<u>ies</u>       party ⟶ part<u>ies</u>
>
> Add an -*s* to nouns ending in a vowel and *y*.
>    monkey ⟶ monkey<u>s</u>     day ⟶ day<u>s</u>

**Practice** Underline the correct plural form of each noun.

1. lady        (ladies, ladys)

2. pass        (passes, pass)

3. brush       (brushes, brushs)

4. party       (partys, parties)

5. tent        (tents, tentes)

6. tax         (taxes, taxs)

7. pitch       (pitchs, pitches)

8. ray         (rays, raies)

**Reteach** • *Plurals (Adding -s, -es; Changing y to i)*

**Plural Nouns** (continued)

On each line, write the word that will complete the phrase. Add -s or -es.

9. ten _____ (kitten)

10. many _____ (hat)

11. four _____ (bus)

12. two _____ (watch)

13. a few _____ (fly)

14. six _____ (toy)

15. two _____ (kiss)

16. five _____ (wish)

Write each word so that it means more than one.

17. patch _____

18. elephant _____

19. lock _____

20. grass _____

21. family _____

**Apply** Write two sentences. In each sentence, use one of the plurals you formed above.

1. _____

2. _____

Name _____  Date _____

# Inflectional Endings

City Lots

**Focus** When you add the *-ed* or *-ing* ending to words that end in *e*, you must drop the final *e*.

- Some base words do not change when the endings *-ed* and *-ing* are added.
    push, pushed, pushing
- When adding the endings *-ed* and *-ing* to a base word that ends in an *e*, drop the final *e*.
    dance, danced, dancing
- When adding *-ing* to a word, if the word has only one syllable and a short vowel sound, double the final consonant of that word.
    run, running
- To identify the base word of a word that ends in *-ed* or *ing*, drop the ending of the word and look at what remains. If you do not recognize the word, see if adding an *e* helps.

**Practice** Look at the pairs of words. Tell what happens to the base word when the ending is added by writing *no change* or *drop the* e.

1. help / helping     _____

2. like / liked       _____

3. gaze / gazing      _____

4. circle / circled   _____

5. fold / folding     _____

Reteach • *Inflectional Endings*

**Inflectional Endings** *(continued)*

Look at the words ending in *-ed*. Write the base word. Then change the word by adding *-ing*.

6. ached     base word: _____

                 add *-ing*: _____

7. matched     base word: _____

                 add *-ing*: _____

8. aimed     base word: _____

                 add *-ing*: _____

9. dipped     base word: _____

                 add *-ing*: _____

10. piled     base word: _____

                 add *-ing*: _____

11. pasted     base word: _____

                 add *-ing*: _____

12. stopped     base word: _____

                 add *-ing*: _____

**Apply** Write a sentence using one of the words that ends in *-ing* above.

_____

_____

_____

Inflectional Endings • **Reteach**

Name _____  Date _____

# Pronoun-Antecedent Agreement

City Lots

**Focus** Pronouns are words that take the place of nouns. Pronouns must agree in number with the nouns that they replace.

- The singular pronouns *I, me, you, he, she, him, her,* and *it* can replace singular nouns.
  Tom has a kite.
  He wants to fly it outside.

- The plural pronouns *we, us, you, they,* and *them* can replace plural nouns.
  The puppy was given to Michael and me.
  The puppy was given to us.

- The possessive pronouns *her, his, its, my, your, our,* and *their* can replace possessive nouns.
  Enrique and Jose's mom will pick them up.
  Their mom will pick them up.

**Practice** Read each sentence. Circle the pronoun that could take the place of the underlined word or words in each sentence.

1. The presents are hidden in the closet.          They     It

2. Mrs. Heiber conducted the experiment.           She      Her

3. My family's favorite restaurant is China Garden.   We      Our

4. Give the new book to Ben.                       he       him

5. Please answer Beth's question.                  she      her

6. Did Jan find the crayons?                       they     them

Reteach • *Pronoun-Antecedent Agreement*                      57

**Pronoun-Antecedent Agreement** *(continued)*

Many of the pronouns in the following sentences are used incorrectly. Circle each incorrect pronoun. Write the correct pronoun above it.

7. Jason is in charge of selling tickets to the play. Him said we should arrive early.

8. The play starts promptly at 7 o'clock. They is nearly two hours long.

9. I can't wait to see Nikki perform. Her plays the part of a cat.

10. Tran and Tamika play mice. They costumes are really cute!

**Apply** Read each sentence. Draw a line through each pronoun that does not agree with the word or words in dark letters that it replaces. Write the correct pronoun above the one you crossed out.

1. **Mrs. Rabbit** gathered carrots. He fed the carrots to the bunnies.

2. **Ralph and Tim** have a pet mouse. He took the mouse to school.

3. **Mr. Angelo** wants to go to the party. It has a present for Beth.

4. **Scott and I** went hiking. She spent the day on a trail.

Name _____  Date _____

# Long Vowel Spellings

*The Boy Who Didn't Believe in Spring*

**Focus** You will be able to spell more words correctly if you know what patterns are used to spell long vowel sounds.

| Long a sounds: | | Long e sounds: | | Long i sounds: | |
|---|---|---|---|---|---|
| *a_e* | cane | *ee* | need | *i_e* | dime |
| *ay* | pay | *ie* | believe | *y* | cry |
| *ai* | aid | *ea* | clean | *ie* | lie |
| | | *y* | sorry | *igh* | light |
| | | *e* | he | | |
| | | *e_e* | theme | | |

| Long o sounds: | | Long u sounds: | |
|---|---|---|---|
| *o* | no | *u_e* | cube |
| *o_e* | stove | *u* | unit |
| *oa* | coal | *ew* | pew |
| *oe* | toe | *ue* | blue |
| *ow* | mow | | |

**Practice** Read each list of words. Draw a line through the word that does not have a long vowel sound.

1. pine, cry, dry, like, hint

2. peek, bet, relief, queen, tease

3. flow, code, cook, globe, moan

4. bait, shake, play, scale, clap

5. cone, rail, wheat, range, purse

6. cake, toe, tail, hole, tug

Reteach • *Long Vowel Spellings*

**Long Vowel Spellings** *(continued)*

Draw lines to match long vowel sounds that follow the same spelling pattern.

7. bike          pupil

8. bone         high

9. bugle         smoke

10. tight         zero

11. taco         flea

12. dream        mice

**Apply** Circle the word in each sentence that has a long vowel sound. For each word you find, write another word with the same spelling pattern.

1. Did Mother bake dessert for us? _____

2. The nail fell on the floor. _____

3. I can see the shed from the porch. _____

4. Jill's dream was fun. _____

5. When will the snow stop? _____

6. The fishing boat was sinking fast. _____

7. Did Pat say something? _____

8. Jen will dig up the weed. _____

9. That is his lucky shirt. _____

10. Ned just found a dime. _____

Name _____  Date _____

# Conjunctions and Compound Sentences

*The Boy Who Didn't Believe in Spring*

**Focus** Use a conjunction to combine two simple sentences into a longer, or compound, sentence.

- A **simple sentence** has only one thought.
- A **compound sentence** is two simple sentences joined with a comma and a conjunction. *And, or,* and *but* are conjunctions.

| | |
|---|---|
| Simple sentences: | Martin read the book. He really enjoyed it. |
| Compound sentence: | Martin read the book, <u>and</u> he really enjoyed it. |
| Simple sentences: | Mr. Wong may drive. He may walk. |
| Compound sentence: | Mr. Wong may drive, <u>or</u> he may walk. |
| Simple sentences: | The book is hard to read. It is interesting. |
| Compound sentence: | The book is hard to read, <u>but</u> it is interesting. |

**Practice** Underline the conjunction in each sentence.

1. Sara got a new bracelet, but she lost it.

2. The bracelet may be at home, or it may be at school.

3. Sara looked in her desk, and there was her bracelet!

Reteach • *Conjunctions*

**Conjunctions and Compound Sentences** *(continued)*

Read each set of sentences. Join the two sentences into a compound sentence by using a comma and the conjunction in parentheses.

4. Sam brought the sandwiches. I brought the lemonade. (and)

    Compound sentence: _____
    _____

5. The peaches came from our tree. We bought the apples at the market. (but)

    Compound sentence: _____
    _____

6. The neighbors' dog plays in our yard. Sometimes he gets into our garbage. (and)

    Compound sentence: _____
    _____

7. Remember to set your alarm clock. You might miss the bus. (or)

    Compound sentence: _____
    _____

**Apply** Write a compound sentence of your own, using a comma and a connecting word.

_____
_____
_____

Name _____  Date _____

# Context Clues

**Urban Roosts**

**Focus** To find the meanings of words you don't know, use context clues.

> When you find a word you do not know in your reading, use its context—the information, words and sentences, around the unfamiliar word—to find out its meaning.
>
> Thomas has a <u>distinct</u> voice. He doesn't sound like anyone I've ever heard before.
> **Clue words:** *doesn't sound like anyone*
> **Meaning:** *not the same, different*
>
> We had <u>abundant</u> food at the campout. We all were stuffed.
> **Clue word:** *stuffed*
> **Meaning:** *great amounts*

**Practice and Apply** Read each set of sentences. Then, read the words below. Circle the word that has the same meaning as the underlined word.

1. Mrs. Frankel was <u>furious</u> when she saw the broken window. I thought she would never stop yelling.

   angry          happy          excited

2. Farmer Jane's pig is very <u>stout</u>. He must eat more food than he needs.

   skinny         fat            hungry

3. The money Mr. Fowler gave was a <u>donation</u>. The school does not have to pay him back.

   gift           loan           check

Reteach • *Context Clues*

**Context Clues** *(continued)*

4. Cleo's pin was very <u>ornate</u>. It was made of green and blue stones in the shape of a pretty flower.

   simple      fancy      plain

5. The mountain climbers were happy when they reached the <u>summit</u>. They left a flag to show they made it all the way up the mountain.

   top      rest area      lake

6. The train <u>departs</u> in fifteen minutes. Buy your ticket now, or you will miss it.

   stops      leaves      travels

Read the sentences. Use context clues to determine the meaning of each underlined word. Write the meaning.

7. I am <u>clenching</u> the kite in my hand. I won't let go.

   _____

8. Grandpa <u>dozed</u> off watching television. He woke up after an hour.

   _____

9. The trail was <u>unfamiliar</u> to me. I did not know the way to go.

   _____

10. The <u>yacht</u> was tied at the dock. It was big compared to the rowboat.

    _____

Name _____  Date _____

# Present, Past, and Future Tense Verbs

**Urban Roosts**

**Focus** Verbs can show that action happens in the present, past, or future.

- **Present-tense verbs** show action that is happening now.
  I <u>eat</u> popcorn at the movie.
  Jeff <u>is eating</u> more popcorn than Ben.

- **Past-tense verbs** show action that has already happened.
  My brother <u>cleaned</u> his room quickly.

- **Future-tense verbs** show action that will happen in the future.
  I <u>will sleep</u> on the couch.

Rules for writing the correct form of a verb:

- If the subject is singular, add *-s* to most verbs. If the subject is plural, do not add an ending to the verb.
  a child listens     the children listen

- Some present tense verbs have special forms.
  be: is, am, are

- Add *-ed* to many verbs to put them in the past tense. Others are irregular.
  train     trained          ride     rode

- Add *will* in front of the verb to form the future tense.

Reteach • *Verbs: Present, Past, and Future Tenses*

**Present, Past, and Future Tense Verbs** (continued)

**Practice** Look at the verb underlined in each sentence. Write *past*, *present*, or *future* on the line beside the sentence.

1. Sarah walked to the park with me. _____
2. I help my father every Saturday. _____
3. I will go to my aunt's house to spend the night. _____
4. Our dog stayed under the house for two hours! _____
5. Mom will cook the vegetables for dinner. _____
6. I play games with my sister all the time. _____
7. We counted six puppies in the basket. _____
8. Sue will sing in the talent show. _____
9. Jane called me last night. _____
10. The baby smiles at everyone. _____
11. The cat pulled the cloth off the table. _____

**Apply** Write the past tense of the verb in parentheses.

1. Tom _____ to the park. (skate)
2. Suzi and Liz _____ the front yard. (rake)
3. We _____ the chocolate chip cookies. (taste)
4. Who _____ the ball in the street? (kick)
5. Marcia _____ the tray to her table. (carry)
6. I _____ a ribbon on the present. (tie)

Verbs: Present, Past, and Future Tenses • **Reteach**

Name _____  Date _____

# Fantasy and Reality

*Make Way for Ducklings*

**Focus** An author may write a story that is based on fantasy or on reality.

- In a **fantasy** story, the people, animals, or objects are able to do things they could not do in the real world.
- In a **realistic** story, the people, animals, places, and events are real or seem real.

**Practice** Read each title. Tell whether each story is based on fantasy or reality.

1. "Journey to the Center of the Earth" _____
2. "A Day at the Office" _____
3. "Elves in the Kitchen" _____
4. "The Wishing Window" _____
5. "My Dog Buttercup" _____
6. "The New Computer" _____
7. "The Flying Cat" _____
8. "A Florida Vacation" _____
9. "At Home with Mr. and Mrs. Mouse" _____
10. "Living Under the Ocean" _____
11. "Jenny's First Day of School" _____

Reteach • *Fantasy and Reality*

**Fantasy and Reality** *(continued)*

Read the list of story events. Write an *R* beside each event that could be part of a realistic story.

_____ 12. Jessica liked her new mountain bike.

_____ 13. A boy fell as he was running to the door.

_____ 14. The dog said he was hungry.

_____ 15. The plane flew above the clouds.

_____ 16. Both frogs flew to the boat.

_____ 17. Larry ran faster than the car.

_____ 18. A family built a playhouse.

_____ 19. Pat took a job as a reporter.

_____ 20. The singing mice also played the piano.

_____ 21. A school has a pet show.

_____ 22. The toys had a midnight party.

_____ 23. The family reunion was held at a park.

_____ 24. The trees in the forest talked about the coming storm.

**Apply** Write two story titles. Make one for a realistic story and one for a fantasy story.

1. realistic: _____

   _____

2. fantasy: _____

   _____

Name _____ Date _____

# Main Idea and Details

*City Superheroes*

**Focus** The main idea of a paragraph tells what the paragraph is about.

- The **main idea** is often, but not always, the first sentence of a paragraph. Placing the main idea first helps the reader know what the paragraph is about.
- The other sentences in the paragraph tell about the main idea. These are called **detail sentences**.
- Sentences can be facts or opinions. **Facts** can be proven true, and **opinions** are someone's thoughts, beliefs, or feelings.

**Practice** Read each sentence. If it is a fact, write an *F*. If it is an opinion, write *O*.

_____ 1. Rosebushes have thorns.

_____ 2. My baby brother is funny.

_____ 3. There are nine planets.

_____ 4. Disneyland is my favorite vacation spot.

_____ 5. Summer has the warmest months of the year.

_____ 6. Kim is ten years old.

_____ 7. Roses are prettier than daisies.

_____ 8. There are seven days in a week.

_____ 9. Our team is the best!

Reteach • *Main Idea and Supporting Details*

**Main Idea and Details** (continued)

**Apply** Read the following main-idea sentences. For each main idea, write one fact and one opinion sentence that will support the main idea. The first one is done for you.

1. All cuts should be bandaged.

   Fact: **Cuts can get infected.** _____

   Opinion: **Old sheets make the best bandages.** _____

2. Trees give shade.

   Fact: _____

   Opinion: _____

3. A good breakfast is important to your health.

   Fact: _____

   Opinion: _____

70    Main Idea and Supporting Details • **Reteach**

Name _____  Date _____

# Fiction and Nonfiction

**City Superheroes**

**Focus** Fiction tells a story about imaginary people and events. It is not true. Nonfiction tells a true story about real people or events.

> - **Fiction** is a **pretend story**. It is not something that has happened. An author imagines the events in a fictional story.
>
>   Examples of fiction:
>   *Charlotte's Web*
>   *Tales of a Fourth-Grade Nothing*
>
> - **Nonfiction** is a **true story** about real people and events. Nonfiction often gives us useful information, like how to do something or the way things work. It can also tell us about the actions of real people or events in history.
>
>   A book about how skyscrapers are built would be nonfiction.

**Practice** Writers of nonfiction rely on facts to explain a subject to the reader. Read each sentence below. Put an *X* through the word or words that don't belong because they aren't facts, according to "City Superheroes." Look back at the story if you need help.

1. Raccoons eat (berries, frogs, fish, rocks, raccoons, and beetles).

2. Raccoons can (chew through, untie) string.

3. Rats like to be active during the (night, day).

4. Rats eat (only cheese, lots of different foods).

Reteach • *Fiction and Nonfiction*

**Fiction and Nonfiction** (continued)

Read each paragraph below. Next to each paragraph, write *N* for nonfiction or *F* for fiction.

_____ 5.   The first roller-skate wheels were made of wood. Metal wheels came later. Now, most people use skates with plastic wheels. The best part about today's wheels is that they can turn you into a person with all kinds of new things to do.

_____ 6.   When the old man went to bed that night, he did as he was told. When he opened his eyes the next morning, he found himself in a cottage with a straw roof and flowers growing up the side. He was very pleased. But he quite forgot about the elf.

_____ 7.   Every year, people in Seattle, Washington, have a wonderful time at Seafair. People come from many places to have fun. One of the most popular parts of the fair is the Milk Carton Derby. In the Derby, people race boats made from milk cartons.

**Apply** Write one nonfiction sentence.

_____

_____

_____

Name _____  Date _____

# Building Vocabulary

**City Superheroes**

**Focus** As readers build their vocabulary, they can learn more and understand more.

> Readers can improve their vocabulary skills in many ways.
>
> - To find out what a word means, ask questions.
> - To learn the meanings of difficult words, discuss the reading selection with others.
> - To discover the meaning of a word, use a dictionary.
> - The author may include definitions in the text.

**Practice** Read each sentence and look for context clues to the meaning of the underlined word. Circle the letter of the correct definition.

1. Uncle Cecil wanted me to <u>tether</u> the horses. So I led our horses to a tree and attached their reins to a limb.

   a. to tie an animal to keep it from wandering
   b. to allow an animal to run freely

2. When I grow up, I want to be a <u>botanist</u>. My mother thinks I would enjoy that because I have always liked working in our garden.

   a. someone who studies animals
   b. someone who studies plants

3. Last night stars shone <u>luminously</u>. I could have read a book from their glow.

   a. darkly      b. brightly

Reteach • *Building Vocabulary*

**Building Vocabulary** (continued)

4. When I broke the window of my father's car with a baseball, I was very penitent. My father said not to feel guilty because accidents happen.

    a.  having a sense of guilt; feeling sorry

    b.  making a mistake

Use a dictionary to write definitions for the following words.

5. mackeral: _____

    _____

6. unique: _____

    _____

**Apply** Read each paragraph. Then, circle the way you would find the definition of the underlined word.

　　Consider the brown rat, for instance, by far the most successful of the two rat species among us. Brown rats have learned a lot since spreading out across the world from their Asian burrows.

a.  use the dictionary
b.  look for definitions the author included

　　They've latched the chicken coops, and the raccoons unlatched them; they've sealed up doorways, and the raccoons came in through the chimney; they've hung sacks of bird food on strings from trees, and the raccoons untied—didn't chew through, *untied*—the string.

a.　look for clues in the text
b.　ask questions

Name _____  Date _____

# Abbreviations

*City Superheroes*

**Focus** Some words can be shortened. They sometimes end with a period. These words are called **abbreviations**.

Abbreviations are simpler ways to write words such as titles, measurements, days of the week, months of the year, and place names. Some abbreviations are followed by a period. Others do not have a period.

| **Titles** | | **Days of the week and months of the year** | |
|---|---|---|---|
| Mister | Mr. | Monday | Mon. |
| Senior | Sr. | Thursday | Thurs. |
| Doctor | Dr. | January | Jan. |
| Junior | Jr. | August | Aug. |

| **Measurement words** | | **Place names** | |
|---|---|---|---|
| foot | ft. | Pine Street | Pine St. |
| cup | c. | Oak Road | Oak Rd. |
| meter | m | New York | NY |
| pound | lb. | New Jersey | NJ |

**Practice** Circle the word in each sentence that could be written as an abbreviation.

1. Cindy lives on Jackson Avenue.

2. The recipe calls for 2 cups of peaches.

3. Jay walks past First Street on his way to school.

4. Doctor O'Brien has puzzles in her waiting room.

5. We bought a pound of cheese.

Reteach • *Abbreviations*

**Abbreviations** (continued)

Look at the word next to each sentence. Write its abbreviation to complete the sentence.

6. Mister       _____ Cortez is my mail carrier.

7. Thursday    Jason's birthday is _____, May 6.

8. Street      I go to school on Harrisburg _____

9. Junior      The winner of the contest was Henry Sloan, _____

10. New Jersey  I live in _____

11. meter      The board is one _____ long.

12. August     Jim went on vacation in _____

13. January    In Montana, it snows in _____

Match each measurement abbreviation with the word it stands for.

14. pound      in.

15. ounce      lb.

16. inch       oz.

17. mile       mi.

**Apply** Write a sentence in which you use an abbreviation in your birth date.

_____

_____

76                                              Abbreviations • Reteach

Name _____   Date _____

# Fact and Opinion

*Sunflowers for Tina*

**Focus** Writers use facts in their writing to give more information. Writers can use facts to support an opinion.

---

**Facts** are details that are known to be true. Facts help to explain a writer's ideas.
 A tulip is a kind of flower.

**Opinions** are what someone thinks or feels. An opinion cannot be proven true or false.
 The daffodil is the most beautiful flower of all.

---

**Practice** Next to each sentence below, write *fact* if it gives a fact. Write *opinion* if it gives an opinion.

1. _____ A dollar is worth one hundred pennies.

2. _____ Reading in bed is bad for your eyes.

3. _____ Tomato juice is red.

4. _____ Classical music is better than rock music.

5. _____ The U.S. flag has stars and stripes.

6. _____ The boy is playing football.

7. _____ Saturday is the best day of the week.

8. _____ Mary lives three blocks from school.

9. _____ The bald eagle is our national bird.

10. _____ I should have a telephone in my bedroom.

Reteach • *Fact and Opinion*

**Fact and Opinion** (continued)

Read each paragraph. Some of the sentences contain facts. Some contain opinions. Find one sentence that is a fact sentence. Put one line under it. Find one sentence that is an opinion sentence. Put two lines under it.

11. Long ago, people made their own candles. They would use them for lights at night. Today, many people use candles, but for different reasons. You can find candles in many shapes, sizes, and colors. I like red candles best!

12. Owls do their hunting at night. They watch the ground with large eyes that seem to glow in the dark. Their eyes look scary. Owls can even hear noises on the ground. When owls hear a mouse or a chipmunk, they can quickly catch it.

**Apply** Write one fact about your favorite holiday. Then, write one opinion about the same holiday.

_____

_____

_____

_____

_____

Name _____ Date _____

# Author's Purpose

*Sunflowers for Tina*

**Focus** An **author's purpose** is his or her reason for writing a story in a certain way.

- The four main reasons for writing are to inform, to entertain, to persuade, and to explain.
- There can be more than one purpose for writing something.

**Practice** Read each sentence. Write *I* if it gives information or teaches you something. Write *E* if it entertains or makes you laugh.

_____ 1. Ashley made the cookies for the bake sale.

_____ 2. The rabbit hid under the shed.

_____ 3. The cow jumped over the moon.

_____ 4. Fish and whales live in the ocean.

_____ 5. The apples and oranges danced under the stars.

_____ 6. The mermaid made the octopus laugh.

_____ 7. Memorial Day is at the end of May.

_____ 8. George Washington was the first president of the United States.

_____ 9. There once was a family who lived in a dollhouse.

_____ 10. Our club is selling popcorn to make money.

Reteach • *Author's Purpose*

**Author's Purpose** (continued)

Read the definitions below. Decide which one fits with the correct sentence. Write the word in the blank.

**explain:** to make clear or understandable

**inform:** to provide information

**persuade:** to convince or lead someone to believe or do something

_____ **11.** Going to the circus would be fun!

_____ **12.** To make a banana split, first cut a banana in half.

_____ **13.** Pioneers traveled west in covered wagons.

_____ **14.** Flying is the best way to travel.

_____ **15.** To plant flowers, first dig up the soil.

_____ **16.** The *Star Wars* movies were made by George Lucas.

_____ **17.** Many different kinds of animals live in the city.

_____ **18.** Try Winkies cereal! You'll love it!

**Apply** Choose as your topic a favorite game, story, or animal. Then, write a sentence that will give the reader information about your topic.

_____

_____

_____

Name _____ Date _____

# Possessive Nouns

*Sunflowers for Tina*

**Focus** Words that show who owns or has something are called **possessive nouns**.

---

- Add an apostrophe (') and -s ('s) to nouns to show that one person owns something.
    the bone of Max
    Max + 's = Max's
    Max's bone

- To make a plural noun show ownership, add an apostrophe.
    the toys of the sisters
    the sisters + ' = the sisters'
    the sisters' toys

- If a plural noun does not end in s, add an apostrophe and -s.
    the stories of the children
    the children + 's = children's
    the children's stories

---

**Practice** Write the possessive form of each underlined noun.

1. the mother of <u>Tina</u>            _____ mother

2. the voices of the <u>men</u>         the _____ voices

3. the newsstand of <u>Mr. Samuels</u>  _____ newsstand

4. the eyes of <u>Grandmother</u>       _____ eyes

5. the seeds of the <u>sunflowers</u>   the _____ seeds

**Possessive Nouns** *(continued)*

Write the possessive form of each noun in parentheses.

6. The (farmer) _____ fields were just plowed.

7. The (workers) _____ faces were suntanned after a long day on the farm.

8. The plants were growing tall in (Mr. McDonald) _____ fields.

9. The (plants) _____ roots were getting plenty of water.

10. The (mice) _____ homes were in the cornfields.

11. The (horses) _____ stalls were in the barn.

12. The (painter) _____ brushes were new.

13. (Jimmy) _____ bike is bright red.

14. Have you read the (girls) _____ stories?

15. The (cat) _____ claws are sharp.

**Apply** Write a sentence using the possessive form of the word.

boys: _____

_____

_____

Name _____ Date _____

# Compare and Contrast

| The Blind Men and the Elephant |
|---|

**Focus** Writers sometimes use **comparison** in a story to make an idea clearer and to make the story more interesting for the reader.

- **Comparing** means to tell how things, events, or characters are alike.
- **Contrasting** means to tell how things, events, or characters are different.

**Practice** Read each sentence. Underline the two things that are being compared.

1. A parakeet sings, but a parrot can speak.
2. A car can go faster than a bicycle.
3. Cheetahs and tigers are both cats.
4. A bird is like an airplane.
5. The sun is like a big ball in the sky.
6. Marshmallows are like soft clouds.
7. Puppies are as playful as kittens.
8. Green beans and corn are both vegetables.
9. A wagon is smaller than a truck.
10. Flowers and weeds are both plants.

Reteach • *Compare and Contrast*

**Compare and Contrast** *(continued)*

**11.** Peas are green, but corn is yellow.

**12.** Apples and oranges are both kinds of fruit.

Look at the sentence comparing a dog and a cat. Tell how they are alike and how they are different.

A dog is like a cat.

**13.** How are they alike? _____
_____

**14.** How are they different? _____
_____


**Apply** Choose two characters from a story you have read. Write their names.

_____

_____

How are these characters alike?
_____
_____
_____

How are they different?
_____
_____
_____

Name _____   Date _____

# Short Vowel Sounds

*The Blind Man and the Elephant*

**Focus** It is important to know the most common short vowel patterns to help spell words correctly.

- The vowel sound in *cat* is spelled *a*.
- The vowel sound in *let* is spelled *e*.
- The vowel sound in *tin* is spelled *i*.
- The vowel sound in *rock* is spelled *o*.
- The vowel sound in *tub* is spelled *u*.

**Practice** Write each word under the correct vowel-sound label.

| bet | rock | cup | mud | pat |
| hop | sit | bad | hit | egg |

**Short *a***
_____
_____

**Short *i***
_____
_____

**Short *e***
_____
_____

**Short *o***
_____
_____

**Short *u***
_____
_____

Reteach • *Short Spelling Patterns (cvc)*

**Short Vowel Sounds** (continued)

Use a word in the box to complete each list. The words in each list have the same short vowel sound.

| net | hip | pop | hat | jug |

1. stop  _____  hop
2. set   _____  let
3. lip   _____  tip
4. cat   _____  rat
5. bug   _____  mug

**Apply** Read the clue to make a new word. Then, use the new word to answer the question.

1. Change the vowel sound of *big* to spell something groceries can go in.

   _____

   What rhyming word describes something used to wipe up spills?

   _____

2. Change the vowel sound of *dog* to something done with a shovel.

   _____

   What rhyming word names a kind of farm animal?

   _____

Short Spelling Patterns (cvc) • **Reteach**

Name _____  Date _____

# Multisyllabic Words

*The Cat Who Became a Poet*

**Focus** Words can be divided into syllables. A syllable is a part of a word said all at once, without pausing. Every syllable has one vowel sound.

- Words vary in the number of syllables they have. Some words have only one syllable.
    name        cat            fish
  Other words have more than one syllable.
    open        spelling       perfectly

**Practice** The following words are divided into syllables. Read them quietly, counting the syllables as you read. Write the one-syllable words on the first line, the two syllable words on the second line, and the three-syllable words on the third line.

| wa / ter / fall | which         | a / gain   |
| lean            | gen / tle     | be / neath |
| show            | re / mem / ber| blow / ing |

One-syllable words: _____

_____

Two-syllable words: _____

_____

Three-syllable words: _____

_____

Reteach • *Multisyllabic Words*

**Multisyllabic Words** *(continued)*

| both | horse | character | recall |
| colder | together | salt | yesterday |
| understand | summer | visit | tray |

Place each word from the box in the correct list according to the number of syllables.

**1**                         **2**                         **3**

_____          _____          _____

_____          _____          _____

_____          _____          _____

_____          _____          _____

**Apply** Read the words below. Beside each word, write the number of syllables.

corner _____          poet _____

beautiful _____          starry _____

slide _____          umbrella _____

respond _____          little _____

telephone _____          trees _____

alarm _____          catnip _____

alphabet _____          dream _____

nap _____          change _____

88

Name _____   Date _____

# Subject and Object Pronouns

*The Cat Who Became a Poet*

**Focus** A pronoun is a word that takes the place of a noun. Pronouns help writers avoid using the same nouns over and over.

- *I, you, he, she, it, we,* and *they* are examples of subject pronouns.
    Frank got a new bat. He used it today.

- *Me, you, him, her, it, us,* and *them* are examples of object pronouns.
    The crowd cheered for her.
    That crayon belongs to him.

- The words *you* and *it* can be either subject pronouns or object pronouns.
    I saw you yesterday.
    You were getting on the bus.

**Practice** Underline the pronoun in each sentence. Then, tell whether it is a subject pronoun (the subject of the sentence) or an object pronoun (found in the predicate of the sentence).

1. She is staying at her cousin's house. _____

2. Rachel let her hold the baby. _____

3. He is going to the park with his parents. _____

Reteach • *Subject and Object Pronouns*

**Subject and Object Pronouns** *(continued)*

4. They are camping at the lake. _____

5. Michelle wants to go with us. _____

6. Mrs. Stevens needs you to help clean the room.

   _____

7. It was the best present of all! _____

8. Susan will help them make dinner. _____

**Apply** Replace the underlined word with the correct pronoun. Then, rewrite each sentence.

1. Kate likes to play ball. <u>Kate</u> plays ball every day after school.

   _____

   _____

   _____

2. I saw the three men riding on horses. Then, I saw the <u>three men</u> get off their horses.

   _____

   _____

   _____

Name _____ Date _____

# Biography

*Picasso*

**Focus** A biography is a story of a real person's life that is written by another person.

- A **biography** has important information about a person's life. It can be about a person's entire life or only an important part. A biography tells the most important things that happened in the person's life.

- A reader can identify a biography by figuring out if the story is about a real person and if it includes facts and information.

**Practice** Read the sentences below. Decide if they could be taken from a biography. Write *yes* or *no* on the lines provided. Then, underline the clues that helped you make the decision.

1. When she was eighty years old, Grandma Moses became famous for her paintings of farm life. She didn't understand why people were so excited about her pictures. She had painted for many years and thought that anyone could paint. _____

2. Thousands of people visit Yellowstone National Park each year. The many geysers and interesting wildlife make the park a favorite place for tourists. _____

Reteach • *Recognize and Distinguish Biographies*

**Biography** *(continued)*

3. Mark Twain wrote *The Adventures of Tom Sawyer* and *The Adventures of Huckleberry Finn.* His own boyhood adventures helped him write these two books. _____

4. The sea lion looked at his sister and said, "What would you like to have for dinner?" She looked at the sea lion. "I am not sure what I want to eat. I am not very hungry." _____

**Apply** Read each paragraph and answer the questions.

    Helen Keller could not see. She could not hear. She could read Braille. She graduated from both high school and college and wrote books.

Is this paragraph a biography? _____

How do you know this? _____

_____

    The largest trees in the world live in the Sequoia National Park in California. These trees are called sequoias. The tallest tree is more than 300 feet high. They are the oldest living trees in the world.

Is this paragraph a biography? _____

How do you know this? _____

Name _____   Date _____

# Spelling Final -le and -el

*Picasso*

**Focus** Certain letter combinations that produce the same sound can be spelled more than one way.

- Many words end with -le.
    bubble, ladle, bicycle
- Some words end with -el.
    funnel, cruel, label
- Because there are no rules to tell you when to use -el and -le, you must memorize the correct spellings.

**Practice** Look at the words in the box below. Place them under the column that matches their ending.

| apple | gravel | maple | model |
|-------|--------|-------|-------|
| bagel | bugle  | camel | fable |

**Words that end with -el**

_____

_____

_____

_____

**Words that end with -le**

_____

_____

_____

_____

Reteach • *Spelling Final -le and -el*

**Spelling Final -le and -el** *(continued)*

Underline the correct spelling of the words in parentheses.

1. A diamond is a type of (jewle, jewel).
2. Bobby will use a (towle, towel) when he gets out of the pool.
3. Susie's (uncle, uncel) is coming to visit next week.
4. *A, e, i, o,* and *u* are all (vowles, vowels).
5. I just finished reading my first (novle, novel).
6. Roberto saw an (eagle, eagel) when he went to the zoo.
7. Connie took a bite out of the red (apple, appel).
8. Drew likes (maple, mapel) syrup on his pancakes.
9. My family will stay at a (hotle, hotel) on vacation.
10. Mom will use a (ladle, ladel) to dish out the soup.
11. There will be a lot of (people, peopel) watching the parade.
12. Debbie got to ride a (camle, camel) at the circus.

**Apply** Choose one of the words from the box on page 93 and use it in a sentence.

_____
_____
_____
_____

Name _____  Date _____

# Author's Point of View

*Roxaboxen*

**Focus** Point of view means who is telling a story.

---

**First-Person Point of View**

- A character in the story is telling the story. The storyteller tells about his or her own thoughts or feelings.
- The storyteller uses the words *I, me, we, our,* and *us*.

**Third-Person Point of View**

- The storyteller is not a character in the story. The storyteller tells about things that happen to other people in the story.
- The storyteller uses the words *he, she, him, her, they, their,* and *them*.

---

**Practice** Identify the point of view in each sentence. In the spaces provided, write *1* for first-person point of view and *3* for third-person point of view.

_____ 1. I remember when I first met Jonah.

_____ 2. Emir thought for a moment, then he turned left.

_____ 3. Kim really liked Miss Temple.

_____ 4. Carol gave the ball to Tim and went home.

_____ 5. When I was three years old, I went to the zoo.

_____ 6. She gave me a watch and told me to wear it always.

**Author's Point of View** (continued)

_____ 7. "What will I do now?" thought Carlos.

_____ 8. I remember my mother always said, "Be sure to eat your vegetables."

_____ 9. I named my puppy Ralphie.

_____ 10. Thanksgiving is their favorite holiday.

_____ 11. I played outside on Saturday.

_____ 12. Our school is on Main Street.

_____ 13. Debbie is going to wash her dog tonight.

_____ 14. Billy wanted to write a school newspaper.

_____ 15. I read the most wonderful book today.

**Apply** Write one sentence from the first-person point of view and one sentence from the third-person point of view.

first-person point of view: _____

_____

_____

third-person point of view: _____

_____

_____

Name _____  Date _____

# Setting

Roxaboxen

**Focus** The time and place in which the events of a story happen are called the **setting**.

- The setting of a story is where the events take place.
- The setting of a story is also when the story takes place.
- The setting of a story may change. Different parts of a story may happen in different places or at different times.

**Practice** Read the stories. Answer the questions that follow each one.

When Rose and her family arrived, the game had not yet started. People were still buying sodas and hot dogs and looking around for their seats. Rose's dad found seats high up in the stands. They watched the players warm up by throwing and catching balls and swinging their bats. The sky looked black and starless behind the bright lights. Rose checked the clock on the scoreboard. "It's almost eight o'clock," she said. "Time to start the game."

1. What clues does the writer give that the story takes place at a baseball game? _____

_____

_____

Reteach • *Setting*     97

**Setting** (continued)

2. Does the game take place during the day or at night?
   _____

Underline the details that help you know when the game took place.

   What a great day we had yesterday! It was sunny and pleasant. My family packed a picnic and went to the zoo. There is a picnic area surrounded by trees. It is very shady. There were so many animals to see. The giraffe and the polar bear were my favorites. I can't wait to go back again.

3. Where does this story take place? _____
   _____

4. What clues tell you where this takes place? ____
   _____

5. When does this story take place? _____
   _____

**Apply** Write one sentence describing the setting of a place you have been with friends or with your family.

_____
_____
_____
_____

Name _____   Date _____

# Commas in a Series

*Roxaboxen*

**Focus** Writers use commas to separate three or more items listed together in a sentence.

- In a series of three or more **nouns**, use a comma after each noun that comes before *and* or *or*.
   The invitation said to bring a bathing suit, a towel, and sunscreen lotion.

- In a series of three or more **adjectives**, use a comma after each adjective that comes before *and* or *or*.
   In the garden, Jane discovered a snake that was long, green, and striped.

- In a series of three or more **verbs**, use a comma after each verb that comes before *and* or *or*.
   The students will draw, paint, or make sculptures of their favorite animals.

**Practice** Look at each pair of sentences. Underline the sentence that has the correctly placed commas.

1. Alex borrowed my skateboard helmet, and knee pads.

   Alex borrowed my skateboard, helmet, and knee pads.

2. I would like a black, blue, or yellow raincoat this year.

   I would like a black, blue or yellow raincoat this year.

3. Please ask everyone to put away their books, paper, and pencils.

   Please ask everyone to put away their books paper and pencils.

Reteach • *Commas with Words in a Series*

**Commas in a Series** *(continued)*

4. Ella, Kate, and Toni can sit in the back seat together.

   Ella, Kate and Toni can sit in the back seat together.

5. Children can swing, slide, or ride the merry-go-round at the new park.

   Children can swing slide, or ride the merry-go-round at the new park.

6. Mrs. Lopez likes to write stories, work in the garden and paint in her spare time.

   Mrs. Lopez likes to write stories, work in the garden, and paint in her spare time.

**Apply** Read each sentence. Then, finish the sentence that follows. Make sure to use commas in the correct places.

1. Eric's three favorite colors are blue, orange, and gray.

   My three favorite colors are _____

   _____.

2. Swimming, jogging, and playing football are Mr. Jackson's favorite sports.

   My three favorite sports are _____

   _____.

3. Moyeesha's four favorite foods are carrots, peanut butter, apples, and green beans.

   My four favorite foods are _____

   _____.

Name _____  Date _____

# Inflectional Endings

**The Bremen Town Musicians**

**Focus** Sometimes the spelling of a base word changes when *-ed* and *-ing* endings are added.

- Drop the final *e* when adding the endings *-ed* and *-ing* to a word that ends in a silent *e*.
    vote        vot**ed**        vot**ing**
- Double the consonant when adding the endings *-ed* and *-ing* to words that have a short vowel sound and end in a consonant.
    stop        stopp**ed**        stopp**ing**

**Practice** Look at the pairs of words. Identify the spelling change that is made to the base word when the ending is added by writing *drop the* e or *double the consonant*.

1. beg / begging          change: _____
2. surprise / surprised   change: _____
3. chat / chatted         change: _____
4. get / getting          change: _____
5. cure / cured           change: _____
6. announce / announcing  change: _____
7. pop / popped           change: _____
8. give / giving          change: _____

Reteach • *Inflectional Endings*

101

**Inflectional Endings** (continued)

**Apply** Look at the words ending in -*ed*. Write the base word. Then, change the word by adding -*ing*. Identify the spelling change you made and write it on the line.

1. hopped

    base word: _____

    add -*ing*: _____

    change: _____

2. moved

    base word: _____

    add -*ing*: _____

    change: _____

3. clapped

    base word: _____

    add -*ing*: _____

    change: _____

4. spanned

    base word: _____

    add -*ing*: _____

    change: _____

5. stated

    base word: _____

    add -*ing*: _____

    change: _____

6. wasted

    base word: _____

    add -*ing*: _____

    change: _____

Name _____  Date _____

# Subject-Verb Agreement

*The Bremen Town Musicians*

**Focus** In a sentence, the verb must agree with the subject. This includes the verb *to be*.

- When the subject is singular, the verb must be singular. When the subject is plural, the verb must be plural.
    Andrew eats lunch at noon.
    Carter and his friends eat lunch at 12:30.

The words *am*, *is*, *are*, *was*, and *were* are forms of the verb *to be*.

- Use *am* or *was* with the word *I*.
    I am ready to go fishing.
    I was looking for my fishing pole.

- Use *is* or *was* with one person, place, or thing.
    Liz is ready to go, too.
    She was already in the boat.

- Use *are* or *were* with more than one.
    The fishermen are ready to leave.
    We were happy to join them.

**Practice** Read each sentence. Then, circle the form of the verb that should be used with the noun.

1. Tyler (was, were) the first boy on the bus.

2. The elephants (is, are) my favorite animals at the zoo.

3. Miguel and Rosa (leave, leaves) for camp in the morning.

4. Jordan (is, are) learning to play the flute.

Reteach • *Subject-Verb Agreement*

**Subject-Verb Agreement** *(continued)*

5. We (work, works) together to clean up the park.

6. I (try, tries) to finish before the bell rings.

7. The three bikes (is, are) red.

8. Two skaters (glide, glides) across the ice.

9. The toad (hop, hops) into the field.

10. Aunt Merrie (live, lives) in California.

11. Sam (was, were) late for class.

12. The sky (is, are) blue.

13. Sally (buy, buys) her lunch everyday.

14. The boxes (is, are) empty.

15. Two kittens (sit, sits) in a box.

**Apply** Complete each sentence with a form of the verb *to be* that agrees with the subject.

1. The students _____ meeting in the cafeteria.

2. Fernando _____ here before the bell rang.

3. We _____ going on a picnic today.

4. My brother _____ in the sixth grade.

5. I _____ born in February.

6. Abby _____ the winner of the Science Fair.

Name _____  Date _____

# Sequence

A Story, A Story

**Focus** The more you know about the time that things happen and the order in which things happen in a story, the better you can understand a story. Writers call this **sequence**.

- Some words tell the **time** or when things happen.
  once     before     tonight
  today     after

- Some words tell the **order** in which things happen.
  first     finally     last
  next     second

**Practice** Read each sequence clue word. On the lines provided, indicate whether each word shows time or order.

_____ 1. later

_____ 2. third

_____ 3. January

_____ 4. last

_____ 5. Saturday

_____ 6. first

_____ 7. today

_____ 8. tonight

_____ 9. finally

Reteach • *Sequence*

**Sequence** (continued)

Underline the time and order words in each sentence.

10. Finally it was our turn to go.

11. We hope to see a movie tonight.

12. Will you be the next to go?

13. Once Tom was in the water, he was fine.

14. I am going on a trip in August.

15. First, Seth put the cake mix in the bowl.

16. Mom took us to the pool yesterday.

17. Tomorrow is Beth's birthday.

18. Next, you spread the jam on the bread.


**Apply** Read each set of sentences below. Number the sentences in each set in the correct order.

_____ Then, she ate her breakfast.

_____ First, Kim turned off her alarm.

_____ Finally, she walked to her school.

_____ Next, she got dressed and brushed her teeth.


_____ On Wednesday, we had spaghetti for dinner.

_____ On Monday, we went shopping for shoes.

_____ On Saturday, we went to the park.

_____ On Thursday, we went to the grocery store.

Name _____    Date _____

# Author's Purpose

*A Tale of the Brothers Grimm*

**Focus** An author's purpose is the author's reason for writing a story in a certain way.

- The author's purpose can be *to inform*, *to explain*, *to entertain*, or *to persuade*.
- An author can have more than one purpose for writing.

**Practice** Read each sentence. Then, write the author's purpose for each sentence. Use the purposes in the box below to help you.

| to inform | to explain |
| to entertain | to persuade |

_____ 1. It is raining outside.

_____ 2. You should not play with matches.

_____ 3. To make toast, put the bread into the toaster.

_____ 4. Grocery stores sell food.

_____ 5. Balloons are usually filled with air.

_____ 6. My homemade rolls are the best in the world.

_____ 7. Buddy was a busy bumblebee.

_____ 8. The lion stood on his head for the crowd.

Reteach • *Author's Purpose*

# Author's Purpose (continued)

_____ 9. To make a cake, begin by gathering all of the ingredients.

_____ 10. Our school is the best in the state.

_____ 11. The sheep laughed when the cow juggled.

_____ 12. The first step in wrapping a gift is to measure the paper.

_____ 13. Plants grow from seeds.

_____ 14. My pumpkin pie tastes better than Betty's.

_____ 15. The cat took the dog for a walk.

**Apply** Identify the purpose of each of the following paragraphs. Write the purpose on the line.

1. New York City is in the northeastern United States. It is one of the world's largest cities. The city is divided into five sections called boroughs.

   _____

2. Mira had never even imagined such a big city! She told her mother that they only had one day to see the sights, so they had better get started right away.

   _____

3. We have the best schools, the best shopping, and the most exciting sports teams. If you are smart, you will drop everything and move here now. What is keeping you living where you are, when you could have all this city offers?

   _____

Name _____  Date _____

# Classifying and Categorizing

*Carving the Pole*

**Focus** **Classifying and categorizing** means putting things into groups.

> Readers sort information into different groups or categories. This helps them to understand and remember what they read.

**Practice** Circle the one thing that does not fit into each category.

1. **Things found at the park**

    swings      slide      lion      trees

2. **Things to drink**

    book      orange juice      lemonade      milk

3. **Things found on a farm**

    tractor      bus      cow      sheep

4. **Things to write with**

    marker      crayon      pencil      buffalo

5. **Vegetables**

    chicken      corn      peas      broccoli

Reteach • *Classifying and Categorizing*

**Classifying and Categorizing** (continued)

The items in the box below can be used for a birthday party. They can be divided into two categories—party supplies and food. Place each item from the box under its correct category.

| ice cream | napkins | birthday cake |
| party favors | punch | balloons |

**Party Supplies**                    **Food**

_____        _____

_____        _____

_____        _____

**Apply** The things listed below might be found at the zoo. Read the words in the box. Think of two categories that might contain these items. Write the categories on the lines. Then, sort the items into their correct category.

| giraffe | soda | tiger |
| popcorn | bear | hot dogs |

Category: _____       Category: _____

_____        _____

_____        _____

_____        _____

Name _____  Date _____

# Spelling: Final *-le* and *-el*

**Oral History**

**Focus** Certain letter combinations that produce the same sound can be spelled more than one way.

- Many words end with *-le*.
    uncle    little
- Many words end with *-el*.
    model    novel
- Because there are no rules to tell you when to use *-el* and *-le*, you must memorize the correct spellings.

**Practice** Write the following words that end with either *-el* or *-le* in the correct list.

| shovel | able | travel | example | purple |
| barrel | freckle | level | apple | vowel |

**Words that end with *-el***

_____

_____

_____

_____

**Words that end with *-le***

_____

_____

_____

_____

Reteach • *Final -le and -el*

**Spelling: Final *-le* and *-el* (continued)**

Underline the correct spelling of the words in parentheses.

1. The student put the (apple, appel) on the teacher's desk.

2. My family likes to (travle, travel) during the summer.

3. Please set a good (exampel, example) for your younger brother.

4. The gymnast had reached the highest (level, levle) of competition.

5. The (purpel, purple) flower is an iris.

6. The students were (able, abel) to complete their homework quickly.

7. The driveway was made out of (gravle, gravel).

8. Marcus read two (novels, novles) over the weekend.

9. The (little, littel) boy was happy to see his dad.

10. Doug always likes to (shovle, shovel) snow in the winter.

**Apply** Read the two words below. Choose one and write a sentence using the word.

puzzle     barrel

Name _____ Date _____

# Types of Sentences

*Oral History*

**Focus** Writers use different kinds of sentences to make stories more interesting.

- A **statement** tells something and ends with a **period**.
    Jeff ate his lunch.
- A **question** asks something and ends with a **question mark**.
    When do you want to go?
- A sentence that shows strong feeling ends with an **exclamation point** and is called an **exclamation**.
    I can't wait for the party!

**Practice** Read each sentence. Write an *S* if it is a statement, a *Q* if it is a question, or an *E* if it is an exclamation.

_____ 1. A long time ago, great-grandfather Ian came to this country from Ireland.

_____ 2. How did he get here?

_____ 3. It was a long and difficult journey!

_____ 4. He crossed the ocean on a tall sailing ship.

_____ 5. Why did he come here?

_____ 6. He wanted a better life, and he found it!

_____ 7. What time is dinner?

_____ 8. Dinner is at six o'clock.

Reteach • *Types of Sentences*

**Types of Sentences** *(continued)*

Read each sentence. Decide whether it is a statement, a question, or an exclamation. Add the correct punctuation to each sentence.

9. A tribal chief in New Zealand had to prove his family really owned their land _____

10. What do you think he did _____

11. How could he prove that they owned the land _____

12. He told the history of his people _____

13. His amazing story took three days _____

14. Imagine that _____

**Apply** Write an exclamation. Be sure to use an exclamation point.

_____

_____

_____

_____

Name _____     Date _____

# Common and Proper Nouns

*Aunt Flossie's Hats*

**Focus** A **noun** is a word that names a person, place, or thing.

- A **proper noun** names a **particular** person, place, or thing. It begins with a capital letter.
- A **common noun** does not name a particular person, place, or thing.

| **Common Noun** | **Proper Noun** |
|---|---|
| city | New Orleans |
| street | Maple Street |
| president | Abraham Lincoln |

**Practice** Decide whether the underlined noun in each sentence is a common noun or a proper noun. On the line, write *common* or *proper*. Then, if the noun is a proper noun, write the noun on the line capitalizing it correctly.

1. The <u>milwaukee county zoo</u> is a fun place to visit.

   _____

2. It is located on <u>bluemound road</u>.

   _____

3. Many <u>people</u> visit the zoo each year.

   _____

4. The children like to visit the <u>elephants</u>.

   _____

Reteach • *Nouns*     115

**Common and Proper Nouns** (continued)

5. Does amy enjoy riding the train around the zoo?

   _____

6. Benjamin visited the zoo last july.

   _____

7. Benjamin's favorite exhibit was the reptiles.

   _____

8. I think benjamin liked watching the crocodiles.

   _____

9. The zookeeper fed the crocodiles.

   _____

10. The crocodiles ate several small fish for lunch.

    _____

**Apply** Write a sentence using the proper noun in the box below.

| San Diego Zoo |

_____

_____

_____

Name _____  Date _____

# Dialogue

> *The Keeping Quilt*

**Focus** Dialogue is the talk between characters in a story.

---

In a story, **dialogue**

- helps to make characters more real by telling how they think and feel.
- helps move the story along.

Writers use **quotation marks** in dialogue to show the reader the exact words of the characters.

Writers use a **comma** to separate the speaker's words from the rest of the sentence.

Writers use a **capital letter** to begin the first word inside the quotation marks.

"Married you'll be someday," Anna told Carle.

---

**Practice** Look at the sentences below. Add quotation marks to show the exact words of the speaker.

1. Those daisies are beautiful! exclaimed Lauren.

2. I think we should pick some for Grandmother, replied Haley.

3. She will love them, added Lauren.

4. Grandmother, we have a surprise for you! called the girls.

5. These flowers are beautiful, Grandmother said.

6. Where did you find them? asked Grandmother.

7. In the field up the hill, said Haley.

Reteach • *Punctuating Dialogue*

**Dialogue** (continued)

Look at the sentences below. Add commas where needed to separate the dialogue from the rest of the sentence.

8. "Mother said to hurry up" said Suzi.

9. Uncle Max said "Tomorrow we are going to the lake."

10. "I am going to go swimming today" said Beth.

11. "What a beautiful drawing" said Mrs. Crotty.

12. John asked Stephen "Can I go with you to the store?"

13. "Eat your vegetables" ordered Father.

14. "I am looking forward to breakfast" said Jennifer.

15. "We have music today" said Mrs. Baca.

Look at the sentences below. Add both quotation marks and commas where they are needed.

16. We are going on a field trip today said Mrs. Walker.

17. Will we be gone all day? asked Billy.

18. We will be back in time to go home said Mrs. Walker.

19. I am very excited! exclaimed Jackie.

**Apply** Pretend you are having lunch with a friend. Write a sentence using dialogue that tells what you would talk about.

_____

_____

_____

Name _____   Date _____

# Making Inferences

*Home Place*

**Focus** Instead of telling readers everything, writers sometimes just give hints. Readers must use what they already know to understand the story.

> Readers can use what they know to figure out details the author left out. Read these sentences.
>
> >Jessica hopped up on the wagon. She held on so tight that her knuckles turned white.
>
> Readers know that when they are afraid of falling off of something, they hold on very tightly. So the clues "so tight" and "knuckles turned white" help to make the inference that Jessica was afraid she would fall off the wagon.

**Practice** Read the paragraph. Then, answer the questions.

>Sam couldn't wait to visit his grandparents. As soon as he arrived, he ran to the field behind their house. Some of the workers were feeding animals. Sam loved to see the cows, hens, sheep, and goats. Other workers were in the large barn. Sam watched Mr. Green plow a large field.

Where do Sam's grandparents live? _____

Write three clues that helped you to know where Sam's grandparents live.

Clue 1: _____

Clue 2: _____

Clue 3: _____

**Making Inferences** (continued)

**Apply** Read the statements. Then, write an inference you might make to explain the situation described in the sentence.

1. You come home at night, turn on the light switch, and nothing happens.

    Inference: _____

    _____

2. You are eating lunch when the phone rings. When you return to the table, you notice that your sandwich is gone and your dog is licking her lips.

    Inference: _____

    _____

3. You are walking on a busy street and you hear a screech of tires and a loud bang.

    Inference: _____

    _____

4. Mark made sure to put the hood up on his raincoat before he went outside.

    Inference: _____

    _____

Name _____  Date _____

## Synonyms and Antonyms

Home Place

**Focus** You can use synonyms and antonyms to make your writing more interesting and to say exactly what you mean.

- A **synonym** is a word that means almost the same thing as another word.
    - cold–icy        sound–noise
    - look–glance     yell–shout
- An **antonym** is a word that means the opposite of another word.
    - all–none        long–short
    - over–under      good–bad

**Practice** Draw a line to connect each pair of synonyms.

1. tired         frighten
2. scare         sleepy
3. speedy        enjoy
4. little        quick
5. like          talk
6. wonderful     terrific
7. speak         mad
8. angry         small

Reteach • *Synonyms and Antonyms*  121

**Synonyms and Antonyms** (continued)

Look at each underlined word. Then, circle the word that is its antonym.

9. beautiful     pretty     ugly
10. everyone     no one     everybody
11. whisper     yell     mumble
12. find     discover     lose
13. friend     enemy     pal
14. nice     kind     mean

**Apply** Write a sentence for each of the words in the box.

| fast | slow |
|------|------|

_____

_____

_____

_____

_____

Name _____ Date _____

# Adjectives and Adverbs

*Home Place*

**Focus** Adjectives are used to describe people, places, or things. Adverbs describe verbs.

> - **Adjectives** are words that describe nouns. They tell how many, what kind, or which one.
>   <u>Two</u> friends met me at the park. (how many)
>   The <u>red</u> truck pulled up to our school. (what kind)
>   <u>That</u> soccer ball is mine. (which one)
>
> - **Adverbs** describe verbs. They tell how, where, or when the action is performed.
>   I walked home <u>slowly</u>. (how)
>   Kathy put the book <u>there</u>. (where)
>   We will be home <u>soon</u>. (when)

**Practice** Circle the adjectives. Then, draw a line from the adjective or adjectives to the underlined noun it or they describe. Some nouns have more than one adjective.

1. Mother gave me three large oatmeal <u>cookies</u>.

2. I have two <u>tickets</u> for the movie tomorrow.

3. Sam caught a shiny, white <u>baseball</u> that was hit over the fence.

4. I ate four hot <u>dogs</u> and drank two <u>sodas</u>.

5. Jenny and I had a wonderful <u>day</u>.

Reteach • *Adjectives and Adverbs*

**Adjectives and Adverbs** (continued)

Circle the adverb that describes the underlined verb. Ask yourself which word tells *how*, *when*, or *where* the action takes place.

6. The dog <u>barks</u> loudly at the mail carrier.

7. Jenna <u>runs</u> faster than I do.

8. Yesterday I <u>lost</u> my favorite coat.

9. My mother <u>walks</u> slowly to the mailbox.

10. I quietly <u>finished</u> my work.

**Apply** Write a sentence using the adjective below and a sentence using the adverb below.

| Adjective | Adverb |
|---|---|
| small | quickly |

_____

_____

_____

_____

Name _____     Date _____

# Spelling Plural Nouns

*A New Coat for Anna*

**Focus** A **plural noun** names more than one person, place, or thing.

- Add *-s* to most nouns to change them to mean more than one.
    month → month<u>s</u>    cowboy → cowboy<u>s</u>
- Add *-es* to nouns that end with *s*, *ss*, *sh*, *ch*, *x*, or *z* to change them to mean more than one.
    pass → pass<u>es</u>    bench → bench<u>es</u>
- To make nouns that end with a consonant and *y* plural, change the *y* to *i* and add *-es*.
    penny → penn<u>ies</u>    cherry → cherr<u>ies</u>

**Practice** Read the sentence and circle the correct plural noun.

1. Maria paints pretty (pictures, pictureses) of the jungle.

2. I saw three birds sitting in the (branchs, branches) of that tree.

3. (Holidaies, Holidays) are some of the most exciting days of the year.

4. Jerry saved his (pennys, pennies) to buy an American flag for the Fourth of July.

5. The Jefferson family enjoyed traveling to different (cities, citys) to see fireworks.

6. Jerry's sister ate two (sandwichs, sandwiches) at the picnic.

Reteach • *Plurals*

**Spelling Plural Nouns** *(continued)*

7. Jerry helped his dad fill all the (glasses, glasss) with lemonade.

8. The children saw three (puppys, puppies) in the park.

9. Several (duckes, ducks) were swimming in the pond.

10. As the family drove home that night, they saw several (lightes, lights) shining from the windows of different houses.

**Apply** Write the word on the line that will complete each phrase. Add *-s* or *-es*.

1. two _____
   (lunch)

2. many _____
   (flag)

3. a few _____
   (box)

4. three _____
   (dress)

5. five _____
   (chair)

6. both _____
   (dish)

7. four _____
   (robin)

8. six _____
   (patch)

Name _____  Date _____

# Irregular Plurals

*A New Coat for Anna*

**Focus** A plural noun is a noun that names more than one person, place, or thing. The plural forms of many nouns are irregular.

---

The spelling of some singular nouns must be changed to make them plural.

| **Singular** | **Plural** |
|---|---|
| foot | feet |
| ox | oxen |

A few nouns have the same singular and plural forms.

| **Singular** | **Plural** |
|---|---|
| reindeer | reindeer |
| moose | moose |
| deer | deer |
| spacecraft | spacecraft |

---

**Practice** Circle the correct plural form of each word.

1. womans    women
2. geese     gooses
3. teeth     tooths
4. childs    children
5. sheeps    sheep
6. mice      mouses
7. trouts    trout
8. feet      foots

Reteach • *Irregular Plurals*

127

**Irregular Plurals** (continued)

Read each sentence. Underline the correct plural form of the word in parentheses.

9. It took six (oxes, **oxen**) to pull the wagon.

10. We saw three (**moose**, mooses) by the stream.

11. I sold many of my old (toyes, **toys**) at the sale.

12. Beverly bought five (**towels**, toweles) at the store.

13. It took three (mans, **men**) to move the tree.

14. Two (cares, **cars**) pass us on the freeway.

15. Many (**people**, persons) waited to see the parade.

16. The park has a lot of (benchs, **benches**) to sit on.

17. The librarian read four (storys, **stories**) to our class.

18. Renee visited four (**places**, placeses) on her vacation.

19. A music staff has five (**lines**, lineses).

20. Seven (trouts, **trout**) are swimming in the stream.

**Apply** Read the following sentences. Write the correct plural form above each underlined word.

The <u>womans</u> took the <u>childs</u> to the park. There they saw <u>gooses</u>, <u>deers</u>, and <u>trouts</u>. While they were eating their lunches, a boy lost two <u>tooths</u>. Before leaving, all the <u>childs</u> put their <u>foots</u> in the fountain.

Name _____   Date _____

# Author's Point of View

> **The Musical Palm Tree**

**Focus** **Point of view** means who is telling a story.

---

**First-Person Point of View**

- The story is told by a character in the story.
- The storyteller uses the clue words *I, me, my, our, we,* and *us*.

**Third-Person Point of View**

- The storyteller is not a character in the story.
- The storyteller uses the clue words *he, she, her, his, him, they,* and *them*.

---

**Practice** Circle the clue words that tell you the point of view in the following sentences.

1. I slowly opened the door to the haunted house.

2. Teresa never forgets to feed her dog.

3. When David left, he forgot his book.

4. It was too cold to swim, so I got out of the water.

5. We are going to the amusement park on Tuesday.

6. Seth is going to walk his dog.

7. It was raining, so Koreen put on her raincoat.

8. I am glad that Joel can come over to play with us.

**Author's Point of View** (continued)

9. They went to the beach last year.

10. I saw a moose during our walk through the woods.

**Apply** Read each sentence. Fill in the circle to tell if the sentence is written from the first-person point of view or the third-person point of view. Underline the word or words in each sentence that help you know the point of view.

1. Early one morning, a magic fairy appeared in my mirror.
   ○ first-person point of view
   ○ third-person point of view

2. She looked everywhere for her homework.
   ○ first-person point of view
   ○ third-person point of view

3. Tim and I held a jumping contest for frogs and grasshoppers.
   ○ first-person point of view
   ○ third-person point of view

4. He couldn't wait to go to school today.
   ○ first-person point of view
   ○ third-person point of view

5. They lived on the third floor of the building.
   ○ first-person point of view
   ○ third-person point of view

Name _____  Date _____

# Commas in a Series

Kids Did It! in Business

**Focus** Writers use commas to separate three or more items listed together in a sentence.

- In a series of three or more **nouns**, use a comma after each noun that comes before *and* or *or*.
    Patty brought fruit, nuts, and juice.

- In a series of three or more **adjectives**, use a comma after each adjective that comes before *and* or *or*.
    The kitten felt soft, fluffy, and warm in my arms.

- In a series of three or more **verbs**, use a comma after each verb that comes before *and* or *or*.
    We swam, ate, and played at the beach.

**Practice** Read each sentence. Add commas where they are needed.

1. You will need glue scissors and markers for art class.

2. Lewis had cows chickens horses and sheep on his farm.

3. The red gold green and brown leaves fell off the tree.

4. Leo plans on doing homework eating dinner and going to bed early tonight.

5. Would you like an apple a banana or an orange?

6. I can do a cartwheel a summersault and a handspring.

7. Randy Chris and Mark are going to play basketball.

Reteach • *Commas in a Series*

**Commas in a Series** (continued)

8. I like to read adventure stories nonfiction books and science fiction stories.

9. Jenny is good in math social studies and science.

10. I saw giraffes elephants and bears at the zoo.

11. The store had a sale on turkey ham and chicken.

12. The card was colored with markers crayons and colored pencils.

13. To mail a letter you need an envelope the address and a stamp.

14. We ate played games and took pictures at the party.

15. Leah likes to draw paint and color pictures.

**Apply** Use each set of three words in a sentence. Remember to include commas.

1. run   jump   skip

   _____
   _____
   _____

2. red   blue   yellow

   _____
   _____
   _____

Name _____  Date _____

# Cause and Effect

*Alexander, Who Used to Be Rich Last Sunday*

**Focus** Understanding cause-and-effect relationships helps readers see why things happen in a story.

---

- An **effect** is what happened. A **cause** is why it happened.
- A **cause-and-effect relationship** is when one event makes another event happen.

---

**Practice** Circle the effect in each sentence.

1. My shirt is dirty because I spilled my soda.
2. Billy broke his leg, so he couldn't roller skate.
3. We are out of milk, therefore I didn't have cereal.
4. Because I'm going to the store, I will pick up some milk for Mom.
5. Caitlin has to go to the doctor, so we need to get up early.
6. Everyone is excited because we're going to the fair tomorrow.
7. Michael is in a new school this year, therefore he should make new friends.
8. We were late for school because the bus had a flat tire.
9. I woke up late, so I missed the bus.
10. Tyler lives far away, therefore I don't see him often.

Reteach • *Cause and Effect*

**Cause and Effect** (*continued*)

Underline the cause in each sentence.

11. Our class won a contest, so we had a pizza party.

12. Our basement flooded because it rained all day yesterday.

13. Ben won the spelling contest because he studied a lot.

14. It was raining, so we could not go on a picnic.

15. Because it was so hot, we went swimming.

16. The book made a loud noise because it fell off the desk.

17. I didn't go to school because it was Saturday.

18. It was bedtime, so I went to bed.

**Apply** Each pair of sentences includes a cause and an effect. Read each pair. Then, combine each into one sentence.

1. Effect: We bought a new one.

    Cause: Our old van broke down.

    _____

    _____

2. Effect: I tripped and fell.

    Cause: My shoelace was untied.

    _____

    _____

Name _____  Date _____

# Contractions

> Alexander, Who Used to Be Rich Last Sunday

**Focus** Sometimes writers use shortcuts when they write.

- A **contraction** is a word made by joining two words. When the words are joined, a letter or letters are left out. An apostrophe (') shows where the missing letter or letters should be.
    He will go with me to the store.
    He'll go with me to the store.

- Below are some word pairs and their contractions:

| Word Pair | Contraction |
|---|---|
| we are | we're |
| I will | I'll |
| they are | they're |
| could not | couldn't |

**Practice** Draw a line matching the words to the correct contraction.

1. They are           He's

2. I am               They've

3. He is              They're

4. She will           I'm

5. I have             She'll

6. They have          I've

Reteach • *Contractions*

135

**Contractions** (continued)

Underline the contraction in each sentence. Write the two words that make up each contraction.

7. They'll pick me up after the movie. _____

8. We're going to the park to play ball. _____

9. Tommy said he'd come home with me today. _____

10. Mom said I couldn't have any candy before dinner _____

Choose a contraction from the word box to replace the underlined words in each sentence.

| I'll | we'll | can't | she'd |

11. Sandy <u>cannot</u> swim in the deep end of the pool. _____

12. <u>I will</u> find the hammer for you. _____

13. Mom said <u>we will</u> come to your house tomorrow. _____

14. Cara said <u>she would</u> take me to the store with her. _____

**Apply** Write one sentence using a contraction.

_____

_____

_____

Contractions • Reteach

Name _____   Date _____

# Possessive Nouns

> *Alexander, Who Used to Be Rich Last Sunday*

**Focus** Words that show who or what owns or has something are called possessive nouns.

---

- To make a singular noun show ownership, add an apostrophe and *s* (*'s*).
    The boy wore a hat.
    The boy's hat is blue.

- To make a plural noun show ownership, add an apostrophe after the *s* (*s'*).
    The boys bought their shoes in the shoe department.
    The boys' shoes are brown.

- If a plural noun does not end with *s*, add an apostrophe and *s* (*'s*).
    The children played in the sandbox.
    The children's sandbox is very large.

---

**Practice** Underline the noun that shows possession in each sentence.

1. Paul's model castle was made of cardboard.

2. The castle's moat had real water in it.

3. Margie's castle was made of clay.

4. The students' castles were on display in the library.

5. The castles were among many other of the library's displays.

Reteach • *Possessive Nouns*

**Possessive Nouns** (continued)

Write the possessive form of each noun.

6. uncles _____

7. aunt _____

8. girl _____

9. Greg _____

10. men _____

**Apply** Read the sentences. Write an answer to each question. The first one is done for you.

1. Grandpa has blue eyes. Whose eyes are blue?

   **Grandpa's eyes are blue.**

2. Tim hears the bird singing. Whose song does Tim hear?

   _____

   _____

3. Tamara sees the cat swish her tail back and forth. Whose tail does Tamara see swishing back and forth?

   _____

   _____

4. The leaves on the trees are changing color. Whose leaves are changing color?

   _____

   _____

Name _____    Date _____

# Drawing Conclusions

**Four Dollars and Fifty Cents**

**Focus** By using clues from the story, readers can draw conclusions about what they have read.

---

- To **draw a conclusion** means to make a statement about a character or event by putting together small details about that character or event.

- A conclusion may not be stated in the text, but it should be supported by examples from the text.

---

**Practice** Read the paragraph. Then, answer the question.

When Marisa left her house in the morning, she looked up at the blue sky. A storm was predicted, but the sun was shining. Now, the sky was filled with dark clouds. Suddenly the wind began blowing. Maria started walking faster. All she was wearing was a cotton jacket. She had forgotten her hat and umbrella at home. In the distance, Marisa heard thunder. Then, she saw lightning flash across the sky.

1. What is happening? _____

2. Write three clues that helped you to draw this conclusion.

   Clue 1: _____

   Clue 2: _____

   Clue 3: _____

Reteach • *Drawing Conclusions*

**Drawing Conclusions** (continued)

**Apply** Read each paragraph. Write a conclusion on the lines that follow.

   Marcia has a horse for a pet. She brushes him, feeds him, and exercises him every day. She likes to read about horses. In art class, Marcia likes to draw horses. She also takes riding lessons.

_____

_____

_____

   Howard was excited. He had never been to Alaska before. Howard finished packing his suitcase. He checked to make sure his plane tickets were in the front pocket. He would need to get a good night's rest tonight, so he wouldn't miss the plane in the morning.

_____

_____

_____

Name _____  Date _____

# Building Vocabulary

*Four Dollars and Fifty Cents*

**Focus** Readers need to build their knowledge of vocabulary words.

> Readers can improve their vocabulary skills in many ways.
>
> - To find out what an unfamiliar word means, **ask questions**.
> - To learn the meanings of difficult words, **discuss the reading selection with others**.
> - To find the meaning of a word, **use a dictionary**.
> - The author may include **definitions** in the text.

**Practice** Read each sentence and look for a definition or clue to the meaning of the underlined word. Underline the correct definition.

1. The cowpokes rode in slow circles around the herd, singing cowboy songs and looking out for stray calves.

    a. a tool for guiding cattle

    b. a person who herds cattle

2. The boy stared glumly at the melting ice-cream bar he had just dropped in the dirt.

    a. unhappily

    b. with great joy

Reteach • *Building Vocabulary*

**Building Vocabulary** *(continued)*

3. Manuel went to a <u>blacksmith</u>, a person who makes things out of hot metal, to ask him to make new horseshoes for his pony, Wildfire.

    a. a person who makes things out of hot metal

    b. a person who likes horses

4. When Mary told me her mother was an astronaut, I had some <u>suspicions</u>, but it turned out to be true. Then I felt bad about doubting my friend.

    a. nice things to say

    b. doubts

**Apply** Read the passage. Write the meanings of the underlined words. Then, write the method you used to find each meaning.

1. Every small town in the old West had its <u>Boot Hill</u>, a cemetery for cowboys.

    Meaning: _____

    Method: _____

2. Richard's <u>shenanigans</u> finally got him sent to the principal's office.

    Meaning: _____

    Method: _____

3. Annie got an "A" in Science and could not wait to <u>gloat</u> about it to her brother, who always made better grades than she did.

    Meaning: _____

    Method: _____

Name _____   Date _____

# Fantasy and Reality

*The Golden Touch*

**Focus** Stories can be about things that are **real** or things that are **make-believe**.

- In a **fantasy,** or make-believe story, people, animals, or things are able to do things they could not do in the real world.
- In a **realistic** story, the people, animals, places, and events are real or seem real.

**Practice** Read the titles. Tell whether each story is fantasy or reality. Write *F* for fantasy or *R* for reality.

_____ 1. "The Land of Toys"

_____ 2. "The Shrinking Girl"

_____ 3. "Our New Car"

_____ 4. "The Mermaid Meets the Dragon"

_____ 5. "Third-Grade Memories"

_____ 6. "A New School for Phil"

_____ 7. "The Mirror That Talked"

_____ 8. "How to Fix a Flat Tire"

_____ 9. "Teaching My Baby Sister to Talk"

_____ 10. "A Day at the Beach"

Reteach • *Fantasy and Reality*

**Fantasy and Reality** (continued)

_____ 11. "Owl and Bear's Shopping Trip"

_____ 12. "My Dog, Fred"

_____ 13. "The Lion Who Lives in the Tree"

_____ 14. "The House in the Sky"

_____ 15. "Learning to Sew"

**Apply** Read each paragraph. On the blank line, write *real* or *make-believe*. Then, list one clue that helped you decide.

1. Saturday morning, Mike and his mother went to the animal shelter. Mike wanted to adopt a dog. Mike's mother thought he should get a small dog, because they live in a small apartment.

   Is this story real or make-believe? _____

   Clue: _____

   _____

2. One morning, the sun forgot to get up. At last the wise owl spoke to his friends. "Someone has to fly high in the sky and wake up the sun."

   Is this story real or make-believe? _____

   Clue: _____

   _____

Name _____    Date _____

# Multiple-Meaning Words

*The Golden Touch*

**Focus** Some words are confusing because they have more than one meaning.

- Some words have different meanings in different sentences. For example, the word *light* can mean "not heavy" or "not dark."
- Sometimes other words in the sentence will give clues to the meaning of the word.
- If you are not able to figure out the meaning on your own, use a dictionary.

**Practice** Read both definitions for each of the following words. Then, read the sentences that follow. Finally, write the definition that tells how the word is used in the sentence.

1. rest    a) to stop action or motion

           b) what is left

           I had to stop and *rest* before I could finish the tennis match.

In this sentence, *rest* means _____.

           Hannah ate part of the pizza and saved the *rest* for later.

In this sentence, *rest* means _____.

Reteach • *Multiple-Meaning Words*

**Multiple-Meaning Words** *(continued)*

2. tart     a) pleasantly sour

           b) a small, fruit-filled pie

The lemonade was *tart* but refreshing.

In this sentence, *tart* means _____.

I chose a strawberry *tart* from the bakery window.

In this sentence, *tart* means _____.

**Apply** Read both definitions for the word below. Then, write two sentences. Use one meaning in each sentence.

can      a) to be able to do so

           b) an aluminum container for food or other products

_____

_____

_____

_____

_____

# Punctuating Dialogue

*The Golden Touch*

**Focus** Quotation marks are used to show the exact words of a speaker.

- Use quotation marks at the beginning (") and the end (") of a speaker's exact words.
    "That is true," said the king.

- Use a capital letter to begin the first word inside the quotation marks.
    He said, "Do they not please you?"

- Use a comma to separate the speaker's exact words from the rest of the sentence.
    "They are not wonderful," sobbed the girl.

- Put the end punctuation mark inside the quotation marks.
    "What would satisfy you?" asked Bacchas.

**Practice** Read each sentence and put quotation marks around the exact words spoken.

1. Stop running in the halls! Mr. James barked.

2. Come here so I can give you a hug, Mom said.

3. My coach said, Don't take your eyes off the ball.

4. Please walk with me to school in the morning, Mary said.

Reteach • *Punctuating Dialogue*

147

**Punctuating Dialogue** (continued)

5. Mom, could you pick me up after my piano lesson tomorrow? asked Jamie.

6. Mrs. Carson said, You have very neat handwriting, Nick.

7. Cousin Irma asked, Would you like to visit me this summer?

8. I would love to visit your ranch, said Mike.

Study the following sentences. Put a *C* after each sentence that is punctuated correctly. Put an *X* after each sentence that is not punctuated correctly.

9. "Watch me run! cried Neil." _____

10. Tashara said, "I can run faster than that" _____

11. Matthew whined, "Why can't I go to the store with you?" _____

12. Help me find my shoes, said Juan. _____

13. "Why aren't you ready for school yet?" Dad asked. _____

14. I asked her if she knew my sister. _____

15. "I want to eat dinner now!" she demanded angrily. _____

16. Donna said she wanted to walk home with me. _____

**Apply** Rewrite the following sentence so that it is punctuated correctly.

Who won the game? my father asked.

_____

_____

Name _____   Date _____

# Short and Long Vowel Sounds

Ox-Cart Man

**Focus** If you know the most common short and long vowel patterns, you will be able to spell more words correctly.

- Sometimes two or three consonant letters stand for separate sounds that are blended together.
  the *scr-* in *scrape*        the *-st* in *wrist*
- A short vowel sound is usually spelled with a consonant-vowel-consonant pattern.
  sat    bend    miss    hop    buck
- A long vowel sound is sometimes spelled with a consonant-vowel-consonant-e pattern.
  bake    bike    note    bone    tale

**Practice** Divide the list of words into categories of words with short vowel sounds and words with long vowel sounds.

| mice | pipe | plot  | skin |
| desk | home | huge  | shut |
| sack | camp | grape | cane |

**Short Vowel Sounds**                **Long Vowel Sounds**

_____  _____          _____  _____

_____  _____          _____  _____

_____  _____          _____  _____

Reteach • *Long and Short Vowel Spellings*

**Short and Long Vowel Sounds** *(continued)*

Write the word from the box that contains the same long or short vowel sound as the other words.

| drum globe stake smile ring |
|---|

1. pile, slime, _____

2. gum, sun, _____

3. pig, big, _____

4. rope, slope, _____

5. rake, sale, _____

**Apply** Write one sentence. Use at least two of the words from the box in your sentence.

| gift rich bank strike broke |
|---|

_____

_____

_____

Long and Short Vowel Spellings • Reteach

Name _____  Date _____

# Abbreviations

*Ox-Cart Man*

**Focus** Some words can be shortened. These words are called abbreviations. Abbreviations often end with a period.

> In an **abbreviation**, letters are left out of the word and, usually, a period is added.
> Sun. (Sunday)   NY (New York)
> St. (Street)   Mr. (Mister)

**Practice** Draw a line to connect each word to its abbreviation.

1. January          p.s.
2. teaspoon         Wed.
3. postscript       Jan.
4. Avenue           Fri.
5. Friday           tsp.
6. October          IL
7. year             Mr.
8. Wednesday        Ave.
9. Mister           Oct.
10. Illinois        yr.

Reteach • *Abbreviations*

**Abbreviations** (continued)

Underline the abbreviation in each sentence. Then, write what the abbreviation stands for on the line.

11. I live on 2323 Redwood Rd. _____

12. Dr. Garcia listened to my heartbeat. _____

13. The recipe reads, "Add 4 c. flour." _____

14. The story begins on p. 27. _____

15. The frog was 5 in. long. _____

16. Draw a circle that is 10 cm across. _____

17. Mary is 4 ft. tall. _____

18. Julia was born on Aug. 18, 1990. _____

19. The next game will be on Fri. at 4 o'clock. _____

20. Mr. Jeffers is my homeroom teacher. _____

**Apply** Circle the mistakes in the sentence below. Then, on the lines that follow, rewrite the sentence correctly.

doctor Black said his birthday was on mon, oct 6th.

_____

_____

Name _____  Date _____

# Fact and Opinion

**Heartland**

**Focus** Writers use **facts** and **opinions** in their writing so readers can better understand their ideas.

- **Facts** can be proven true.
    *Michael Jordan played basketball.*
- **Opinions** cannot be proven true or false.
    *Michael Jordan was the best basketball player of all time.*

**Practice** Read each sentence below. Underline it if it gives a fact. Circle it if it gives an opinion.

1. Spiders have eight legs.
2. There are fifty-two weeks in a year.
3. Cats have fur.
4. Muffins are delicious to eat.
5. Bears hibernate in the winter.
6. Beverly Cleary is a great author.
7. Baseball is played in Japan.
8. Thanksgiving is the fourth Thursday of November.
9. Chocolate milkshakes are better than ice-cream sodas.
10. Summer is the best time of the year.

Reteach • *Fact/Opinion*

**Fact and Opinion** (continued)

Read each paragraph below. Find a fact sentence in each paragraph and circle it. Find an opinion sentence in each paragraph and underline it.

11.  Trees grow from seeds. They have limbs that grow from the trunk. Leaves grow on the limbs. Some trees grow fruit. Some trees grow nuts. Trees are very interesting to study.

12.  Dodoes were very unusual birds. Dodoes once lived on the island of Mauritius in the Indian Ocean. A dodo was as big as a large turkey. Their wings were very tiny. Dodoes could not fly. These birds no longer exist.

**Apply** Read the following fact. Now, rewrite it as an opinion.

Swimming is a sport.

_____

_____

_____

Name _____  Date _____

# Figurative Language

**Heartland**

**Focus** Writers use figurative language to help readers picture what is being described.

---

Simile, metaphor, and personification are types of figurative language.

- A **simile** compares two things that are not alike by using *like* or *as*.
    Rebecca's smile was <u>as</u> bright <u>as</u> sunshine.

- A **metaphor** compares two things that are not alike, without using *like* or *as*.
    Rebecca's <u>smile</u> was <u>sunshine</u>.

- **Personification** gives human qualities or characteristics to something that is not human.
    The <u>wind</u> <u>sang</u> in the trees.

---

**Practice and Apply** Read the passage. Circle each example of a simile and underline each example of personification. Then, choose one example of each and answer the questions on page 156.

It was just my luck that the grumpy old school bus broke down. I was as unhappy as a wet cat as I walked to school in the snow. All the way there, the angry wind tried to blow me down. It was a good thing I remembered to wear my new boots. My feet were as warm as toast.

Reteach • *Figurative Language*

155

**Figurative Language** *(continued)*

1. Example of a simile: _____
   _____
   _____

2. Which two things are being compared? _____
   _____
   _____

3. How are they alike? _____
   _____
   _____

4. Example of personification: _____
   _____
   _____

5. What is being personified? _____
   _____
   _____

6. What are the human qualities or characteristics given?
   _____
   _____
   _____

Name _____  Date _____

# Pronouns

Heartland

**Focus** A **noun** is a person, place, or thing.
**Pronouns** are words that take the place of nouns.

> A singular (one) pronoun takes the place of a singular noun.
>> Jennifer lost **the book**. Jennifer lost **it**.
>> **Roberto** is not here. **He** is not here.
>
> Plural (more than one) pronouns take the place of plural nouns.
>> **Anita and Maria** are on the track team.
>> **They** are on the track team.
>
>> Luke has **your shoes**. Luke has **them**.

**Practice** Read each sentence. Write the pronoun that best fits the meaning.

1. The doctor took my sister's temperature, but found nothing wrong with _____.

2. The two friends talked for a while and worked out _____ differences.

3. The dog played with the bone and then buried _____.

4. Finally, the girl finished _____ homework and went outside to play.

5. The children ate dinner as _____ talked about their school project.

6. Sara said, "Please give the book to _____."

Reteach • *Pronoun-Antecedent Agreement*  157

**Pronouns** (continued)

Underline the pronoun in each sentence. Circle the noun or nouns that each pronoun replaces.

7. Betsy lost her kitten.

8. Mark placed his book on the table.

9. Mary and Katie live in that building. They are sisters.

10. This window is stuck. Please close it.

11. Kyle is ready. When will Uncle Bill meet him?

12. Did Max bake the cake? It is good!

13. The books are about animals. They have lots of pictures.

14. Will Mike and Liz drive when they take a trip?

**Apply** Look at the pronouns below. Circle the ones that are singular. Underline the ones that are plural. Then, use at least one of the pronouns in a sentence.

| me | she | it | they | him | we |
|----|-----|-----|------|-----|-----|
| us | her | them | their | he | his |

_____

_____

_____

Name _____  Date _____

# Context Clues

**Cows in the Parlor**

**Focus** To help you find the meanings of words you don't know, use context clues.

> When you find a word you do not know in your reading, use its context—the information, words, and sentences around the unfamiliar word—to find out its meaning.
>
> Thomas has a <u>distinctive</u> voice. It doesn't sound like anyone I've ever heard before.
>
>  **Clue words:** doesn't sound like anyone
>  **Meaning:**  not the same, different
>
> We had <u>abundant</u> food for the campout. We were all stuffed.
>  **Clue word:**  stuffed
>  **Meaning:**  in great amounts

**Practice** Write a definition for each underlined word. Use context clues to help you.

1. The classroom was <u>frigid</u>, so I put on my sweater.

   _____

2. The music was <u>earsplitting</u>. I don't know why it was turned up so loud.

   _____

3. Trying to keep up with the group, he walked <u>briskly</u>.

   _____

Reteach • *Context Clues*

**Context Clues** (continued)

4. My baby brother likes to <u>demolish</u> my toys. I try to remember to put them away so that he cannot destroy them.

   _____

5. Margaret was <u>enthusiastic</u> about seeing the play, unlike Julio, who was not so excited about it.

   _____

6. The <u>buds</u> on the trees will soon open up. The leaves will be green when they open up.

   _____

7. The <u>island</u> was beautiful. The water surrounding it on all sides was crystal clear.

   _____

8. Sheryl's joke was <u>hilarious</u>. I thought I would never stop laughing.

   _____

**Apply** Write one sentence using a word you defined in the Practice exercise.

_____

_____

_____

Name _____   Date _____

# Conjunctions

**Cows in the Parlor**

**Focus** Use a conjunction to combine two simple sentences into a longer sentence.

> Conjunctions can be used to "connect" two or more nouns, verbs, adjectives, phrases, or sentences.
>
> - To join two sentences that contain related ideas, the word *and* may be used.
>   > Bill studied his spelling *and* math.
>
> - To join two sentences that contain opposite ideas, the word *but* may be used.
>   > George fed the cat, *but* it was not hungry.
>
> - To join sentence parts that give a choice, the word *or* may be used.
>   > We can play tag, *or* we can go inside and play a board game.

**Practice** Read the sentences below. Underline the conjunctions.

1. In the summer, Mr. Riddle and the farmers cut the grass.

2. The cows will eat the grass, but they also need corn to make good milk.

3. The Riddle family will eat supper early or wait until after the cows are milked.

4. The hauler pumps the milk into his tanker truck and takes it to the creamery.

5. The milk is made into butter, cheese, ice cream, and yogurt.

Reteach • *Conjunctions*

**Conjunctions** *(continued)*

Underline the two short sentences that were combined to make each sentence.

6. The rain poured, and the wind howled.

7. The boys can run, or they can swim.

8. The pizza is good, but it is hot.

9. The party was fun, and I liked my gifts.

10. Soon we can go, but we must clean up first.

**Apply** Read each pair of sentences. Use a conjunction to put each pair together.

Maggie's calf is light brown. The calf has dark brown eyes.

New sentence: _____

_____

The wind was cold. The snow was cold.

New sentence: _____

_____

The sky was blue. The clouds were gray.

New sentence: _____

_____

Name _____   Date _____

# Making Inferences

*Growing Up Amish*

**Focus** Instead of telling readers everything, writers sometimes just give hints. Readers must use what they already know to understand the story.

> Readers can use what they already know to figure out details that the author left out. Read this sentence.
>     Gwen put on her gold crown.
>
> A reader knows that a queen or princess would have a gold crown. So the clue "her gold crown" help the reader make the inference that Gwen is probably a queen or princess.

**Practice** Read each statement below. Write the inference you can make from each statement.

1. Dogs make the best pets.

   Inference: _____

   _____

2. Camping is too much trouble.

   Inference: _____

   _____

3. Leaves from the vegetable garden had been eaten.

   Inference: _____

   _____

Reteach • *Making Inferences*

**Making Inferences** *(continued)*

4. It was hard to cook hot dogs over the campfire.

   Inference: _____

   _____

5. We took the subway to get downtown.

   Inference: _____

   _____

6. The keeper told the class about what bears eat.

   Inference: _____

   _____

**Apply** Read the paragraph below. On the lines that follow, make an inference about what is happening in the paragraph.

   The rain started coming down in sheets. Everyone ran for cover. The workers covered the field with plastic. The players returned to their dugouts. The fans started going to their cars.

_____

_____

_____

Name _____   Date _____

# Compound Words

*Growing Up Amish*

**Focus** Using compound words can make your writing more interesting.

> A compound word is one word made of two words joined together.
>
> note + book = notebook        a book for taking notes
>
> wind + storm = windstorm      a storm of wind
>
> corn + bread = cornbread      bread made of corn

**Practice** Find two words from the underlined part of each sentence that can be joined to create a compound word. Then, write the compound word.

1. Maria stopped to tie <u>the laces on her shoe</u>.

    word: _____

2. My brother sleeps in the <u>room with a bed in it</u>.

    word: _____

3. The post office worker placed the letters in a <u>box for mail</u>.

    word: _____

4. The farmer liked to ride on <u>the back of a horse</u>.

    word: _____

5. <u>The light of the day</u> begins when the sun rises.

    word: _____

**Compound Words** (continued)

6. My coat is in the room for the class.

    word: _____

7. Jeff went to the corner to get a paper full of news.

    word: _____

8. When we went to the ocean, I saw a fish that looked like a star.

    word: _____

9. Anne will need to take her brush for paint to art with her.

    word: _____

10. My little sister likes to play in the box full of sand.

    word: _____

**Apply** Underline the compound word in each sentence. Then, write the two words that form the compound word.

1. We went sailing in the afternoon.    _____  _____

2. Baseball is Bruce's favorite sport.    _____  _____

3. The bulldog jumped out of the car.    _____  _____

4. My cupcake fell on the floor.    _____  _____

5. The watermelon is in the cooler.    _____  _____

6. My toenail needs to be clipped.    _____  _____

Name _____     Date _____

# Verbs

*Growing Up Amish*

**Focus** Verbs can show that an action happens in the present, past, or future.

- Verbs can show that an action happens in the **present**.
    The class *starts* now.
- Verbs can show that an action happened in the **past**.
    Yesterday we *walked* to the store.
- Verbs can show that an action is going to happen in the **future**.
    We *will eat* in an hour.

**Practice** Underline the verb in each sentence. Then, underline *Past, Present,* or *Future* to indicate the tense used in the sentence.

1. Amish girls wear long skirts.

    Past    Present    Future

2. Everyone rises at 5:00 A.M.

    Past    Present    Future

3. The boy helped his sister with the chores.

    Past    Present    Future

4. He will learn to help in the fields.

    Past    Present    Future

Reteach • *Verbs: Present, Past, and Future Tenses*

**Verbs** *(continued)*

5. After eighth grade, the children will leave school.

   Past     Present     Future

6. The girl swept the kitchen floor.

   Past     Present     Future

7. The men will plow the corn tomorrow.

   Past     Present     Future

8. The children went to school in the fall.

   Past     Present     Future

9. The women wash the clothes.

   Past     Present     Future

10. The girls will learn to sew next month.

    Past     Present     Future

11. The corn was planted in March.

    Past     Present     Future

12. The family walks from the barn to the house.

    Past     Present     Future

**Apply** Write a sentence that tells what you do at school during recess. Use a verb in the present tense.

_____

_____

_____

Name _____  Date _____

# Homonyms

*Just Plain Fancy*

**Focus** Words that sound alike but that are spelled differently and have different meanings are called **homonyms**.

Below are some common homonyms.

| | | | |
|---|---|---|---|
| ate | eight | I *ate* lunch early. | We have *eight* puppies. |
| blue | blew | The sky is *blue*. | The wind *blew* my hat. |
| right | write | Turn *right* at the corner. | I can *write* my name. |
| there | their | Sit over *there*. | *Their* house is new. |
| two | too, to | I have *two* cats. | It's not *too* late *to* go home. |
| for | four | Sam was late *for* class. | I have *four* brothers. |

**Practice** Draw a line connecting the word to its definition. Place an *X* through each of the four homonyms that do not belong.

1. nose
2. ate
3. knows
4. eight
5. sew
6. eye
7. so
8. I

a. a number that comes after seven and before nine

b. stitching with a needle and thread

c. a part of the face used to smell

d. a part of the face used to see

Reteach • *Homonyms*

169

**Homonyms** (continued)

Use the spelling hints below to help you choose the correct homonym to complete each sentence.

**Meat** or **Meet?** Look at the word m<u>eat</u>. You can see the word <u>eat</u>. So you might *meet* your sister, but you would eat *meat*.

9. I will _____ you later.

10. I like _____ in my chili.

**Dear** or **Deer?** If something is *dear* to you, you would like to have it n<u>ear</u>. Did you notice the similar spelling? But if it is a *deer*, it should stay in the woods!

11. The baby _____ was beautiful.

12. My mother calls me her _____ child.

**Hear** or **Here?** Remember that you h<u>ear</u> with your <u>ear</u>.

13. Tasha asked, "Did you _____ me?"

14. Sit _____ so I can take your picture.

**Apply** Use the words *to* and *too* in one sentence.

_____

_____

_____

Name _____  Date _____

# Subject and Object Pronouns

*Just Plain Fancy*

**Focus** A pronoun is a word that takes the place of a noun. They can help you to avoid using the same noun over and over again in your writing.

- *I, you, he, she, it, we,* and *they* are examples of subject pronouns.

    Bob went to practice. He had to be there at two-thirty.

- *Me, you, him, her, it, us,* and *them* are examples of object pronouns.

    Tamara is coming with me.
    Grandfather will visit us next week.

- The words *you* and *it* can be either subject pronouns or object pronouns.

    The teacher told you.
    It was a fun trip!

**Practice** Underline the subject pronouns and circle the object pronouns.

1. She told the class to follow her.

2. They followed her to the lunchroom.

3. He usually has a snack with the rest of us.

4. We liked having the new students sit at the table with us.

5. She couldn't believe him.

6. She picked the apples then cooked them.

7. We need to paint it.

Reteach • *Subject and Object Pronouns*

**Subject and Object Pronouns** (continued)

8. He will now perform a famous juggling act for you.

9. He has to take me to the store today.

10. She is going to walk home with them.

Fill in the blank with a pronoun to complete the sentence.

11. _____ is running with _____ in the park.

12. _____ told _____ the silly story.

13. _____ is broken.

14. Would you like to play with _____ today?

15. If _____ hope to win the talent show, _____ must practice the song.

**Apply** Rewrite each sentence below, replacing each underlined word with a pronoun.

Sarah held baby Anna carefully while Jeff warmed the milk.

_____

_____

_____

Steve asked what time the movie started. Steve was afraid of being late.

_____

_____

Name _____  Date _____

# Multisyllabic Words

**The Country Mouse and the City Mouse**

**Focus** A syllable is a word or word part that contains a vowel sound.

- Some words have only one syllable.
  *both*    *late*    *cold*
- Other words have more than one syllable.
  *summer*    *button*    *almost*

**Practice** Read aloud the following words from the story "The Country Mouse and the City Mouse." Tap your fingers softly with each syllable. Then, write each word in the correct list.

| honest | friend | invited | quantity |
| conversation | overpowered | carpet | set |

**Words with 1 Syllable**

_____

_____

**Words with 2 Syllables**

_____

_____

**Words with 3 Syllables**

_____

_____

**Words with 4 Syllables**

_____

_____

Reteach • *Multisyllabic Words*

**Multisyllabic Words** (continued)

Read aloud each of the following words. Listen to the ending sound of the **first** syllable. Decide whether it ends with a vowel sound or a consonant sound. Then, write the word in the correct list. The first one is done for you.

| | | | |
|---|---|---|---|
| be•long | mem•ber | un•cle | ham•burger |
| la•ter | el•bow | re•main | tri•angle |

**Vowel Sound**

belong

_____

_____

_____

**Consonant Sound**

_____

_____

_____

**Apply** Write one sentence about the area where you live. Include at least three words that have more than one syllable. After writing the sentence, circle the words that have more than one syllable.

_____

_____

_____